The Filmviewer's Handbook

To
Linus J. Thro, S.J.

The
Filmviewer's Handbook

by
Emile G. McAnany, S.J.
and
Robert Williams, S.J.

(An Original Deus Book)

DEUS BOOKS
PAULIST PRESS
(Paulist Fathers)
Glen Rock, N. J.

Contents

Copyright © 1965 by
The Missionary Society
of St. Paul the Apostle
in the State of New York

Library of Congress
Catalog Card Number: 65-21764

Cover Design: Claude Ponsot

Published by the Paulist Press
Editorial Office: 304 W. 58th St., N. Y., N. Y. 10019
Business Office: Glen Rock, New Jersey 07452

Printed and Bound in the
United States of America

24

Foreword

The publication of this compendium of information about starting film study groups is a welcome addition to the little that is already available. Certainly in the past decade, movies have achieved sufficient recognition as a medium of artistic expression to merit serious attention by the widest possible public. In other countries, films have for many years been an accepted part of the total cultural scene. It is therefore surprising that so few American attempts have been made to provide the necessary practical background for those interested in knowing how to show and discuss films intelligently. This book will help overcome the many vexing problems encountered by those beginning such programs for the first time.

Teachers especially should find much valuable material within its pages. In Europe, the film society movement led to the eventual establishments of film education programs in the school. In our own country, film study clubs will likely be the first step towards the incorporation of film classes in the curriculum. In fostering such a development, this volume will be of much help. It is hoped that many schools will use it to initiate their own particular study of the film.

HENRY HERX
National Center for Film Study

Acknowledgments

The authors wish to acknowledge the help that was given during the research and writing of this book.

Mr. Thomas J. Brandon generously allowed the authors the use of the film library of Brandon Films, Inc.; and Miss Jane Welch, who heads the film library, took time from her busy schedule to answer questions and see that various films were made available for us. The Communications Department of Fordham University was kind enough to open their facilities for our research. We would also like to thank the officials of the American Federation of Film Societies for providing much helpful information.

Mr. Henry Joubert, S.J. and Rev. Denis E. Daly, S.J. made many helpful suggestions in the course of the composition of this book. Our thanks, too, to Mr. Richard F. McCaslin, S.J. and the members of the Agency for Jesuit Writers of St. Mary's College who helped prepare the manuscript for publication.

Finally, the authors wish to thank Rev. Phillip Cunningham, C.S.P., for his many helpful suggestions and professional assistance in preparing the final draft of the manuscript.

Introduction

A stroll through a gallery or the casual hearing of a symphony can be entertaining for one who has little knowledge of either painting or music. Similarly, the motion picture is a source of enjoyment to a vast audience who has little appreciation of the art of the film. But, just as the gallery and the symphony are far greater sources of enrichment for the student of painting and music, so the motion picture is more rewarding for those who study the art of the film.

We have chosen to cast the format of this book in terms of a handbook, because this seemed the best approach to use in organizing the material we felt should be included in this work. We have not attempted to make this a comprehensive history of cinema, a treatise on film aesthetics or a textbook of film technique, though we have given attention to these areas insofar as they are necessary for background. The fundamental value of this book will be found in its presentation of information designed to forward the organization and development of motion picture study.

The serious student of the motion picture labors under a handicap. Numerous art galleries are at the disposal of the student of painting. The great masterpieces are readily available in reproduction. Similarly, the concert hall, the radio, and the phonograph rec-

ord aid the student of music. But the student of the
motion picture has no such advantage. If he is to see
one of the great film masterpieces, he must rely on
the "art theater". These are few and their programming must attract an audience sufficiently large to be
commercially successful. A film study group or film
society offers a solution to this problem.

But because very little has been written concerning
formation and continued operation of film societies,
the film society movement in America has tended to
be an individual operation with little or no sharing of
information.

In an attempt to overcome this deficiency, the American Federation of Film Societies was formed in April,
1955. The general purpose of the AFFS is "to serve
its members as a clearing-house of information and
ideas". It aims at "coordinating the efforts of its
members to maximize the benefits of film exhibition,
lectures, literature and other media". While it is also
interested in assisting the formation of new film societies, the impact of the Federation in this area is still
to be felt. At present the influence and value of the
AFFS, while unquestionably important, is restricted
mainly to already existing members. As it continues
to grow and to extend its influence, however, the AFFS
will play an important role in developing interest in
and appreciation of motion pictures.

Since the authors consider the film society to be a
place for serious film study, we have tended to present
what might be thought to be an ideal to be worked
for rather than to be practically expected. We believe,
however, that the ideal will soon be realized; and we
are eager to take part in this movement. Considerable
space has been given to techniques of film discussion
and programming. A sample series has been given and
detailed program notes have been worked out. Other
series have been suggested in brief, and suggestions

for other series have been given. Although we are fully aware that many societies today do not hold discussions in conjunction with their showings nor do they program their series toward some definite goal, we feel this is essential to the notion of a film society and is the trend film societies are now working toward.

Where film titles have been cited we have also included the date of production. This has been done because we feel it absolutely necessary to keep a picture within its historical context. The viewer must remember that movies are ever developing both in treatment of subject matter and technique. An historical view is not only important for a proper understanding of the movies in general, it is also quite important to be able to place a particular film of a director in the total development of his work.

Finally, some word should be given to the authors' conception of their audience. While we are fundamentally concerned with those who wish to increase their appreciation of the motion picture, we have tried to be of particular help to those who desire to organize or participate in a film society or study group. By film study groups we have in mind college and university film societies who want to be more than 16mm "art theaters", independent film societies, church groups, women's clubs and business and professional organizations who, by means of some kind of organized viewing of movies, desire to add to their knowledge and appreciation of the motion pictures. Further, it is possible that this handbook can be used by secondary and college teachers who are trying to add movie appreciation classes to their schools either as regular classroom material or as an extra curricular activity.

On the one hand we have tried not to take anything for granted as far as a beginner might be concerned, while, on the other hand, we have tried to include information that would help already existing societies to improve their operation.

We hope, then, that this will be a source book to be consulted often with profit by its readers.

I
A Compendium of Motion Picture History

The development of motion pictures from a feeble, plaything-like character at the turn of the century to the highly complex medium of entertainment and information seen today is a subject for interesting and fruitful study. Though this book cannot even begin to develop the history of the film in any full sense—as a glimpse at the number of books devoted to film history mentioned in the bibliography will show—still it is important for the beginner of film appreciation to have some idea of the important moments of cinema history. This chapter is intended, then, as a survey to provide the student with a starting point, a point of reference, as it were, for the comments and suggestions that will be made later in the book. It is hoped, of course, that the film student will make the history of the film a subject for his further study.

The movies taken for granted at the local theater or shown commercial-riddled on the television are the product of a long, fruitful—and sometimes not so fruitful—affair carried on between technology, art and economics. Like her sisters in the family of electronic communication, motion pictures are the result of the great nineteenth-century surge of mechanical inventions. But, unlike other mechanical devices whose inventions were the results of obvious needs, the self-starter for example, the movies suffer from the problem of having been invented first before any need for their existence had been established.

Early Days

Though it remained until the late 1800's for motion picture making and projecting to emerge from the scientist's laboratory in any practicable device, the notion of motion pictures is an ancient one. By coupling the realization of the physiological fact that it takes a fraction of a second for the eye to record the impression of an image and then transmit it to the brain and that, having received the impression, the eye retains it one-twentieth to one-tenth of one second after the image has disappeared (the principle known as the persistence of vision) with his inventive imagination, man has performed some amazing, though perhaps primitive, experiments in the illusion of movement. The *Magia Catoptrica* ("magic lantern"), the stroboscope, and the zoetrope ("wheel of life") are examples of the crude though effective experiments conducted as early as the fifteenth century.

For the movies to reach a recognizable level with the motion pictures shown today required the work of the Frenchman Louis Daguerre who around 1839 developed a process whereby a photograph could be exposed on a chemically coated plate. With the invention of photography and the subsequent refinements in the photographic process, it was not long before men began to experiment with the idea of motion picture photographs. Any standard book on the history of film will give the reader names and examples of the many experiments carried on in this area. For the present it will suffice to turn to the work done at the Edison laboratory.

In an attempt to add further refinements to the already invented phonograph, Edison and his assistant William Kennedy Dickson turned their attention to designing an instrument capable of presenting moving pictures to accompany the sounds of the phonograph.

Dickson's work led him to the discovery of motion picture film whereby pictures were reproduced on chemically coated celluloid. In this process, Dickson used a one-and-one-half inch strip of celluloid that afforded space for a one inch picture with room along the edges for sprocket holes that held the film while it passed through the stop-motion device of the camera. The celluloid film used by Dickson was too stiff to make the movie machine practical; but with George Eastman's invention of a thin, flexible film, all that was essentially needed to make a machine for taking and reproducing motion pictures was at hand. The camera was called the "kinetograph" and the viewing machine was called the "kinetoscope". The basic Greek word *kine*, which means motion, is still used today when the movies are referred to as the cinema.

Americans were not the only ones working on inventions designed to capture life by means of motion pictures. In France the names of Louis Le Prince and the Lumiere brothers, Auguste and Louis, are the most significant. Robert Paul and William Friese-Greene are the important names in England. And in Germany Max Skladanowski perfected a machine patterned upon the principles of the kinetoscope which he called, as Paul called his, the "bioscope".

In the beginning, the makers of these motion picture instruments saw no real lasting or commercial value in their inventions. These inventors, consequently, did not bother to get patents on their machines with the result that the camera and projective devices were copied both directly and with slight modifications throughout Europe and America. When, ultimately, the commercial value of these machines was discovered, there began the history of legal battles that for one reason or another has become a lasting part of movie making.

Furthermore, since the makers of these machines

had no interest in the artistic and economic potentials involved in their devices, it remained the job of
new groups of men to discover practical means of production and distribution of the movies.

Commercial Beginnings

It was in France on December 28, 1895, in a base-
ment room in the Grande Café that the public first
encountered the motion pictures emancipated from the
individual peep-show box and projected upon a screen.
The program offered by the Lumiere's through their
cinematograph was a series of short films each about
fifty feet in length and running a few minutes. The
subject matter of the ten films shown that day covered
such varied topics as *Lunch Hour at the Lumiere Factory, Arrival of a Train at a Station,* and *Baby's
Lunch.* This enterprise was under the direction of Antoine Lumiere, the father of Auguste and Louis. Perhaps Antoine Lumiere should be given credit for in-
venting the economic nature of the movies since he
charged an admission of one franc for this showing
and took in the handsome sum of thirty-five francs.

In America the work of Edison reached the public
through the enterprise of Albert Bial. Edison's vita-
scope had its premiere at the Koster and Bial Music
Hall on April 23, 1896. Since Koster and Bial's was
an already popular theater, the audience for this
showing was much larger than the one attracted by
the Lumiere's. The program shown that evening, like
the Lumiere's, was made up of several short films.
The great triumph of the evening was that of waves
breaking on a sandy beach near a stone pile. At the
sight of rolling waters and foam the audience broke
into cheers. The affinity between audiences and the
"magic shadows" experienced by those present in the
Music Hall is still seen in neighborhood theaters
throughout the world.

Now all ingredients are present: machines capable of recording and reproducing action, enterprisers realizing the commercial potential of the movies and enthusiastic audiences willing to pay for the chance to be entertained by an image projected upon a white screen. Only one more element needed to be developed: subject matter that would appeal to large numbers of persons. This, of course, was not long in coming.

Audience Reception

In the early days movies were known as "flickers". Shown in penny arcades and makeshift storerooms, for the most part they were short pictures, the average length running about ten to fifteen minutes, made with crude equipment, presenting simple plots and situations with staged episodes improvised on the spot. The audience was composed of the lower class workingman and his family. Animals and hawkers roamed up and down the aisles contributing their noise to the clatter of the projection machine and the catcalls of the cash customers whenever the film broke, which it did with regularity. It was just this side of bedlam, still the audience loved it for its new and different kind of entertainment. The audience, though heavily weighted to the lower side of the economic scale, numbered among its members the children of the middle and upper classes. For these boys to see a "flicker" was an adventure like sneaking up to the attic to read a *Nick Carter Detective* or smoking a cigarette in some out-of-the-way alley. But, all things considered, the movies in these early days were not the place for "good" little boys.

By 1903, however, the movies had achieved sufficient popularity with a steady audience to make expansion feasible. The period from 1903 to 1908 served to establish the motion picture industry; and the movies became a large permanent business with production, distribution and exhibition as its three different parts. When, in 1905, the first "nickelodeon" was built, the movies began to move uptown, as it were. Pictures began to last for a half hour up to a full hour and ran continuously all day. Production boomed, and speed and quantity became of prime importance.

Pre-World-War-I Developments

From 1908 to 1914 the movie business was marked with bitter competition for the control of the medium. When, after a long antitrust suit, the battle beween the independent producers and the movie combines came to an end in 1917, things began to level off.

The years of competition resulted in better quality films and the years preceding the First World War saw great strides in the development of production techniques.

Since pictures speak an international language, movies enjoyed by American audiences in the early days were drawn indiscriminately from all the film producing countries of Europe. Trick and historical films were imported from France, spectacles from Italy and melodramas from England.

The sun and warmth to be found in California made it a natural place for movie making; so the center of picture production shifted from the East coast to the West and Hollywood, the "movie capitol" of the world, was born.

The years 1908 to 1918 saw the American film develop that unique personality that would lead the American movie to dominate the screens of the world. The directors whose names stand out as the creative

geniuses of this period are D. W. Griffith, Thomas
Ince and Mack Sennett. The individual personality of
each man gave his pictures their own particular bent,
yet men and pictures had in common a display of
creative imagination and tremendous vitality. Comedies of Sennett, westerns of Ince and dramatic studies
of Griffith were exciting exercises in movie making.
For these men the important goal was found in their
experimentation into the technical resources of the
film and the manipulation of the film's emotional
content.

The influence of these men was not restricted to
their fellow American film makers; it spread across
the ocean to cause excitement and admiration where-
ever their films were shown. The pre-World-War-I
period in Sweden, for example, shows the influence of
Griffith and Ince upon the great Swedish directors
Victor Sjostrom [known later in America as Sea-
strom, *Wind* (1928)] and Maurice Stiller, *The Treasure of Sir Arne* (1914) and *The Story of Gosta Berl-
ing* (1924). The Swedish film makers, however, were
not mere imitators of the American directors, and they
had their own unique contributions to give to the development of motion pictures. They are remembered
for their ability to draw characters and themes from
their national literature and then transform them to
make them important for audiences beyond the Scan-
danavian borders. It has been said the Swedish film
was first to depict individual human character with
amplitude and truth, thus teaching the movies how to
suggest motive and mood.

The distinguishing characteristic of film production
in the days prior to World War I, whether in the
United States or in Europe, was the vitality and
imagination of the film makers. By present-day standards, much of what was produced in those early days
is primitive and naive; still the enthusiasm displayed

by the early film makers gives their films a charm
and aesthetic delight that can still be enjoyed today.

World War I

The war years were extremely important in the
history of the movies. It was a period of transition,
wherein the economics, content and influence of the
film were completely changed. In these brief four years
the movies became not only a big business, but a national institution as well. While ravages of war in
Europe brought movie production to a halt on the
continent, Hollywood, free from the restrictions of
battle, became virtually the only source of movie production. The works of D. W. Griffith, *Birth of a Nation* (1915), *Intolerance* (1916) and *Hearts of the
World* (1917), were greeted as real works of art. In
order to accommodate the sensibilities of the upper
classes, special theaters were constructed to show his
pictures. Most of the movies of this period, in keeping with the cultural values of the ever-expanding audience, preached strict late Victorian moral attitudes.
The values of love and marriage and womanly virtue
were extolled, compensations for poverty were end-
lessly dramatized and the good life was patterned on
the experiences of the middle-class members of the
audience.

During this period screen credits were introduced
for the first time. Prior to this time the audience was
attracted by the prestige factor of the company name.
One went to see a particular picture because it was
produced by Essany, Biograph, Vitagraph or Edison.
As the medium began to grow, emphasis began to
shift from action for its own sake to the importance
of "the story". Characterization was established
mainly through dress and decor, with the result that
the actor himself possessed very little personal integ-

rity in the overall production of a motion picture. As the years passed, however, movie patrons began to express their preference for this or that actor although as yet they were actors without names. The patrons would refer to these actors in the following ways: the "Biograph girl", "Imp girl", "Vitagraph boy", or according to their screen names: "Little Mary", the "Husband", the "Banker", the "Waif", or according to some physical trait: the "Girl with the Curls", the "Thin Woman", the "Man with Sad Eyes", and so on. The manufacturers paid no attention to the requests for the names of favorite players, reasoning that any public recognition of the actors would only lead to their demanding higher salaries. In the early days none of the film producers was shrewd enough to see that this mounting interest on the part of the movie enthusiasts could be turned to his own advantage.

It was Carl Laemmle, head of IMP the leading independent company, who made the first "star". Ever on the lookout for some means by which he could attract customers away from his rivals, he acquired the exclusive services of Florence Lawrence, the "Biograph girl", one of the most popular actresses of the day. He offered her the advantages of higher salary and opportunity for widespread publicity. By means of a publicity stunt he brought her to the public attention, a practice which has been imitated with varying successes by many film producers ever since.

With the institution of the star system names like John Bunny, Charlie Chaplin and Mary Pickford were enough to attract huge audiences to view their latest films and to read the exploits of their private lives. At this time fan magazines came into being to exploit the private lives of the movie people; and, incidentally, this was the time when the film critic made his appearance in the daily newspapers and weekly magazines.

Post World War I

After the war the movie industry on the continent began again with a renewed vigor. The war itself and the consequent political and economic turmoil that naturally followed after the armistice caused considerable changes in the European industry. While countries that had been important before the war shrank in importance, others took their places. The British, for example, curtailed in their film making during the war had turned to the American film to fill the gap. The British audience, won over by the fast pace of the pictures coming from the new world, was not at all satisfied with the outpourings of the home studios. Though the British government established a film quota system in the attempt to insure some market for the native product, it was not at all successful; and the British film industry settled into an obscurity from which it did not return until the mid-thirties.

The Scandinavian film industry also suffered a decline after the First World War. This was not caused from the influence of the American film upon the audience but from the gradual migration of the film makers to other countries. America lured Sjostrom and Stiller from Sweden, while Germany drew heavily upon the directors, scenarists, cameramen and actors of Denmark. Important names like Carl Dreyer, *The Passion of Joan of Arc* (1928) and Urban Gad and his wife, the actress Asta Neilson, came to be more associated with the Berlin studios than their own homeland.

The Classical Age

Still, all was not decline in Europe; the postwar film in Germany centered its attention upon psychological and experimental subjects. Such directors as

Murnau, *The Last Laugh* (1924), Dupont, *Variety* (1925), and Pabst, *Secrets of a Soul* (1926) created pictures that revealed new depths in film technique and theory. The credit for the quality productions of this period however does not belong solely to the directors. Contributions of the talented scriptwriter Carl Mayer and the imaginative work of the cameraman Karl Freund, along with the sensitive acting of such men as Emil Jannings and Conrad Veidt, spurred the popularity and influence of the German film abroad.

Just as the Danish film studios had been stripped by the German, so too the German industry suffered the loss of its talent by the lure of American dollars. Directorial greats such as Lubitsch, Leni, Lang and the already mentioned Dupont and Murnau left Germany to take up residence in Hollywood. The plunder of the German studios was not restricted only to the directors. The exodus of German talent was swollen by top writers, actors and cinematographers who sought the moneyed positions awaiting them in America.

The twenties saw a tremendous advance in movie making in Russia. Spurred on by the interest of no less a person than Lenin himself, the film makers in Russia sought new techniques to spread the message of Communism to the masses. Although such directors as Eisenstein, *Potemkin* (1925), Pudovkin, *Mother* (1926), and Dovzhenko, *Arsenal* (1929) produced films of great power and aesthetic beauty, the influence of the Russian film theory and technique did not extend itself to the film makers in America as did that of the Germans. Unfortunately the constant pressures brought to bear upon the movie makers in Russia by political forces caused the great potentials seen in the films of the twenties to become dulled by the weight of propaganda.

From the earliest days, film making in France was taken quite seriously and was considered a respectable medium through which a man might seek to express himself. Men like Dulac, Gance and Epstein sought to create true cinematic experiences as opposed to the traditional stage-influenced movie. The productions of these men were impressionistic in technique and highly romantic in tone. The passage of time has not dealt too kindly with their films, however, since they strike the modern audience as too artificial and precious. Nevertheless, their contributions to the general attitudes of French intellectuals to the film is of real importance in the history of French cinema.

The early works of Rene Clair, *Entract* (1924), Luis Bunuel, *Un Chien Andalou* (1928) and Jaques Feyder, *L'Image* (1925) produced during this period show the influence of the impressionists. More importantly, these films gave indication of the potential of their major works that followed during the age of sound.

Important as the contributions of the German, Russian and French films of the silent period were, it was still the American film that dominated the world film audiences.

American Movies of the Twenties

The impact of the First World War did not affect the European film industry only; the American film also underwent radical changes in the postwar period. The Victorian values that had hitherto been the foundation of the American movie gave way to a wise-cracking sophistication. The wayward husband, the vamp and the long-suffering wife were laughed out of existence; and in their place Cecil B. DeMille dished up a sexual potpourri calculated to appeal to the peripatetic farm boy home from the war. All that was epitomized in such labels as "The Roaring Twenties" and "Flaming Youth" found treatment in such films of the day as *Don't Change Your Husband, Forbidden Fruit* and *Male and Female*. During these turbulent days the movies joined with the press and the theater in the trend of "keeping up with the times" which meant doing as much as possible to reflect the fast changing moral standards of the day.

There is much evidence that during the "golden age" of the silents there were men of integrity and imagination residing in Hollywood. They were not, unfortunately, the men in charge of establishing studio policy or choosing the content of the pictures. The growing cost of movie making had turned Hollywood into a big time enterprise. Movies were called "products" and were the result of assembly-line production of the movie "industry". The heads of the studios and their representatives, the producers, were businessmen, not artists. They were responsible to investors—more and more these had become New York banking interests—and were, consequently, only interested in turning out a "product" that would give a high return on the investment. There is probably no greater factor in keeping the motion pictures from realizing its artistic potential than the fact that the ultimate decisions in the making of a movie are often made by men who have no particular knowledge or talent regarding the movies themselves.

Problems of Censorship

As interest in the movies grew among the masses, every possible method was employed to make the uninitiated become active contributors at the box office. Plush theaters were constructed, reams of material flowed from the pens of press agents chronicling intimate details of life in the movie colony, and stories calculated to have the widest appeal were culled from any possible source as subject matter to be filmed. Competition between the film producers was at an extreme and "anything goes" became the watchword.

Provocative as the content of these movies might have been, it was their blatant advertising that finally led to attempts at reform. The policy of movie producers was to title and advertise all their pictures on the basis of sex, even those pictures which of themselves were quite harmless.

In addition to the poor story content and advertising, two other factors contributed to the loss of prestige of the American film. First, the competition between the businessmen involved in the movie industry became a source of bad publicity through the charges and countercharges fought out in the press and in the courtroom. Secondly, the sensationalism with which the press treated the private lives of prominent movie people began to boomerang. High living, frequent divorces and occasional scandals of a more serious nature brought feelings of disgust to the once ardent public. Even those who were not themselves moviegoers began to form strong opinions concerning the state of the movies and those employed in making them.

The consequence of all this was naturally a demand by many that something be done to reform Hollywood and the movies. Ministers and their congregations, clubwomen, schoolteachers and others met to bring pressure upon the movie industry. Letters were written, committees were formed, and state and federal legislators began to talk in terms of censorship.

Probably no other business is so dependent upon the force of public opinion as is the motion picture industry. Therefore, in order to protect itself from government control and to try to repair the losses at the box office, the big men of the industry called in

Will Hays to create a self-censoring board. The Hays Office succeeded in satisfying neither the outraged public nor the movie producers. It merely limped along issuing periodic communiques to the press indicating that the office was doing all that was possible under the circumstances. Since what the Hays Office was trying to accomplish had no precedent, the final evolution of the Motion Picture Production Code and the Production Code Administration took over ten years of continuous struggle. An unfortunate aspect of the Code as it was finally worked out was that it failed to take into account the possibility of audience maturation. What might have been a socially provocative theme in the early thirties, miscegenation for example, does not have the same effect on audiences today. As the years passed, those film makers who adhered closely to the approved subjects of the Code were beginning to use the Code as an excuse for producing bland pictures. Another group of producers made a game of the Code and used untasteful suggestiveness to get around the restrictions. Still others decided to sidestep the Code altogether and produced films without the Code seal of approval. These men preferred to pay a fine for their violations and used the very fact that their film did not have Code approval as a point of advertising. Fortunately the Code has been revised to a sufficient degree that serious film makers can now make films that are worthy of the attention of more mature moviegoers.

At the same time that the movie industry was establishing the Hays Office, certain private agencies were also setting up film rating programs. The National Legion of Decency, The Green Sheet and the National Board of Review are examples of the work carried on in this area. Of these private groups, the Legion of Decency and The Green Sheet have steadily improved their approach to film classification so that they serve a very useful purpose in the overall development of the American motion picture industry.

The Coming Of Sound

As the 1920's drew to a close the major studios found themselves in serious financial difficulty. Because the novelty of moving pictures had worn out, large numbers of the movie audience were beginning to look elsewhere for their diversion. In an attempt to stop the leakage at the box office, the studio executives began to look about for some gimmick that would again capture the imagination of the masses. The answer to the dilemma, it was suggested, might well be solved by adding sound to the pictures. This answer was quite logical since tinting and other coloring processes had been in use for some time causing color to lose its striking effect. The gimmicks to be seen later in change of size and shape of the screen had not yet been imagined. So sound with the possibility of adding dialogue to the pictures seemed to be an ideal solution.

The idea of combining sound and pictures goes back to the very beginnings of motion pictures. Dickson's attempt to join the picture of the kinetoscope with the already-existing Edison phonograph was not carried out because the financial backers of the kinetoscope desired to exploit the possibilities of moving pictures themselves.

To speak of silent pictures is really not quite accurate since the movies almost from the very first public showing were always accompanied by some kind of musical background whether by a solo piano or a full-scale symphony orchestra with music composed especially for a particular film. And often enough certain sound effects were used to add a certain realism to the movie. The important factor involved in the change from the silent movie to the sound movie, then, was the addition of the spoken word. But this was not so easy to achieve as one might think.

The first major attempt to use a mechanical device as the source of sound was employed by Warner Brothers as a means whereby an orchestral accompaniment could be supplied more inexpensively. The financially ailing Warner Brothers took over the developments of the Bell laboratories in the use of recorded discs designed to last as long as the picture reel. They called this process Vitaphone and introduced it to give the symphonic background to their 1927 production of *Don Juan*. A difficulty arose with this process, however, in the synchronization of the picture to the sound since any breakage, with the consequent shortening of the film, would result in a discernible difference between the picture and the sound. The public did not take to this new process; so it was soon abandoned.

In order to overcome the disc synchronization problem, a scientist named Lee De Forest began to experiment with the idea of putting the sound on the film itself. This process of translating sound into a line of various widths and shades, which when passed through the beam of a photo-electric cell can be retranslated into music and speech, is still the fundamental method used in the making of sound motion pictures.

At first the De Forest process was reserved for the most part to short subjects. The acts of certain vaudeville comedians were put on sound film and shown along with the silent feature during an evening program. Novel as all this was, the audiences were not too impressed. When the Fox Movietone News, using the De Forest process, began to present newsreels of important current events such as the Lindbergh celebrations and interviews with noted personalities, the sound movie really began to capture the imagination of the audience. Yet sound in a feature film did not gain the support of the mass audience until Al Jolson appeared in *The Jazz Singer* (1927).

The transition from silent movies to sound was made with remarkable urgency. All the movie makers were eager to cash in on the box office revival. Procurement of sound mechanism both to film and then to project was a costly enterprise however; so during this period the Eastern financial interests finally completed taking over motion picture financing. To this day the money to be invested in motion picture production remains in the hands of Eastern bankers who, from their offices far removed from the scene of film production, issue their instructions through their agents, the studio heads.

The sound revolution struck Hollywood with all the chaos revolutions are wont to create. Established directors and actors found themselves out of work as new armies of workers, whose training in the theater made them necessary, trooped into California. The microphone began to dominate the camera and all the wonderful techniques of motion developed during the silent period were sacrificed for sound. Instead of showing something, the movies now merely talked about it. The filmed stage play became the common staple in the movie theaters. In the minds of many, the introduction of speech to the motion pictures brought to an end the glory of the movies and forever reduced the movies to a mere two-dimensional imitation of the stage.

Development of the "Talkies"

Bad as things were for the moment, men of talent and imagination were able to break the tyranny of the microphone over the camera. Movies were again produced with the picture holding the dominate position and sound used as a helpmate. Lubitsch [*Love Parade* (1929)], Vidor [*Hallelujah* (1929)], and Milestone [*All Quiet on the Western Front* (1930)] experimented with sound, editing to produce a balance between sound and picture that was something unique in itself and not merely imitation of the stage.

New subjects were opened up for treatment. The musical ranged from grand ballroom spectacles [*Love Me Tonight* (1932)] through musical reviews [*Footlight Parade* (1934)] to the more intimate style of Rogers and Astaire [*Top Hat* (1934)]. Comedians who had the ability to get off a wise crack were imported from the vaudeville stage. Although much of this comedy became dialogue heavy, still there were men like the Marx brothers, Laurel and Hardy, W. C. Fields, Hope and Crosby, and many others who learned to maintain a visual vitality in their pictures.

The gangster film [*Little Caesar* (1930), *Public Enemy* (1931), *Scarface* (1932)], drawing its interest from the daily headlines, was ideally suited to the sound movie because of the short phraseology and rapid speech of the characters presented. The techniques of storytelling developed in the gangster cycle helped to improve the overall presentation of speech in the film melodrama. Screen writers were learning how to pare away unnecessary speech in order to allow the pictures themselevs to do the communicating.

As America moved into the depression, the social, political and economic problems of daily living began to be reflected in the movies. A direct approach to these problems was treated in such films as *I Am a Fugitive from a Chain Gang* (1932), *Black Legion* (1936), *Fury* (1936), *Dead End* (1937) and *The Grapes of Wrath* (1940). Pictures that dealt with life in foreign lands [*The Informer* (1935) and *The Good Earth* (1937)] were also concerned with social problems. Even the comedy of the thirties was colored by the social and economic problems of the day. Some of the memorable comedies of this period were: *It Happened One Night* (1934), *Mr. Deeds Goes to Town* (1936), *You Can't Take It With You* (1938), and *Modern Times*, Chaplin's classic on the problems of automation.

Another popular series during this period was the biography picture. It is noteworthy that the more outstanding pictures produced during this cycle dealt with men whose lives were outstanding because of their social consciousness (Zola, Pasteur, Juarez, Erlich, Reuter, and Abraham Lincoln).

Although there were many good films produced during the thirties, by far the largest bulk of pictures produced were either of a vapid cinderella theme or were melodramas designed to allow the masses escape from the problems of daily living. The attitude of the major producing studios remained what it had been during the silent era. They wanted to make as much return on the investment as possible; so the subject matter and treatment of the majority of the movies was restricted, for the most part, to exploiting by means of subject cycles any popular success. Proven successes from other media, especially the novel and the theater, were also exploited.

European Sound Movies

The problems of changing from silent to sound motion pictures were not restricted solely to the United States. The major film producers in Europe realized that they too would have to switch over to sound pictures if they were to maintain any competition with the American film market. As in America the huge costs involved in changing over to sound production were met by financiers outside of the movie industries themselves. These businessmen, like their American counterparts, were interested in exploiting the renewed audience interest in the movies. This attitude led, of course, to a policy of turning out as many pictures as possible. Quantity rather than quality became the policy of the day.

The language barriers and the poor quality of these films made their export to the United States unfeasible, with the result that knowledge of the pictures produced during this dark period are known to Americans more by hearsay than by actual exposure. But not all of the production in Europe during the thirties was poor. Fortunately there were enough significant films made to keep alive the spirit of imaginative film making on the continent and, consequently, to allow Americans the opportunity to maintain their interest in European film making.

The transition to sound in France was aided immeasurably by the talents of men already established during the silent era. Rene Clair, whose *Italian Straw Hat* (1927) was a great international success, joined sound to his vivid pictorial imagination to produce a series of social satires in such pictures as *Under the Roofs of Paris* (1930), *Le Million* (1931), and *A Nous la Liberté* (1932). In 1938 he went to Britain where he made *The Ghost Goes West*, a comedy well-received in America as well as in England. Clair spent the war years in America where he turned out four pictures.

Jean Renoir, whose talent for translating the works of novelists to the screen was displayed during the twenties, brought the novels of Flaubert [*Madame Bovary* (1934)] and Zola [*La Bête Humaine* (1938)] forcefully to the screen. The interest in naturalism shown in the novelists Renoir chose to film is displayed in the pictures based on other sources and on original screen plays. *Toni* (1934), *Le Crime de M. Lange* (1935), *Le Grande Illusion* (1937) and *La*

Regle du Jeu (1939) are outstanding examples of
Renoir's talent for satire and social commentary. Like
Clair, Renoir also spent the war years in America
where his talents found outlet in films dealing with
the South.

The avant-garde tradition of the French film found
an exceptional talent in Jean Vigo whose *A Propos de
Nice* (1929), *Zero de Conduite* (1932) and *L'Atlante*
(1934) comprise the body of his work. Although
Vigo died at the age of twenty-nine in 1934, the influence of his personality is still felt by many of the
young film makers at work in France today.

The period between the two world wars, especially
during the period of the thirties, produced a unique attitude of fatalism in France that found expression in
such films as Julien Duvier's *La Belle Equipe* (1936),
Pepe le Moko (1936), *La Fin du Jour* (1939); Marcel Pagnol's *The Baker's Wife* (1938) and *The Well
Digger's Daughter* (1940); and Marcel Carne's *Jenny*
(1936), *Quai des Brumes* (1938) and *Le Jour se Lève*
(1939).

As important as the directors were during this period the talents of such screen writers as Charles Spaak
and Jacques Prevert and actors such as Raimu, Jean
Gabin, Michael Simon, Arletty, Michele Morgan and
François Rosay should not be overlooked in the development of the particular approach to film making
that was found in France during the thirties.

In Germany the early days of sound saw the continuation of the psychological themes so popular during the silent period. Lang in his *M.* (1932), Von
Sternberg in the *Blue Angel* (1930) and Pabst's *West-
front 1918* (1930) show imaginative and quite advanced use of sound techniques. As the influence of
Hitler began to be felt throughout Germany, the freedom of film makers began to undergo more and more
restrictions. With the exception of the work of Leni

Reifenstahl (the Nazi propaganda films *Triumph of the Will* and *Olympiad*), the German film industry of the thirties and early forties produced little more than sentimental melodramas and comedies.

Political control in Russia during the thirties also resulted in the lowering of the artistic potential of the film makers. The vacillation of the party line from emphasis on the communal hero to the individual hero caused many films to be scrapped before they could be completed. While it cannot be denied that the Russian film was designed to carry out Lenin's command that motion pictures were to be used as a tool to further political ideology, it would not be true to think of the Russian film only as a vehicle for propaganda. The film technique and acting displayed in such pictures as *The Gorky Trilogy* (1938-40), *Chapayev* (1934), *Shors* (1939), *We Are From Kronstadt* (1936) and *Alexander Nevsky* (1938) enables them to be seen and appreciated by audiences of different political orientation.

The age of sound opened in England with Alfred Hitchcock's *Blackmail* (1929). Originally produced as a silent picture and released in some places in a silent version, it was so constructed that sound dubbing was not difficult. The imaginative use of dialogue and background sounds displayed a talent that Hitchcock would develop more cleverly in years to follow. Sound became the important factor in re-establishing British movies in American theaters. Since the depression caused a decrease in the number of films produced in Hollywood, it was only natural that American theater owners would fill the gap with English language pictures from Britain.

Unfortunately, like the American producers, British film makers began to produce photographed stage plays; so the initial promise of sound movies in England settled for a period into unimaginative theatrical reproductions. Perhaps the most important British movie of the thirties was Anthony Asquith's *Tell England* (1931). Dealing with the Gallipoli landings during the First World War, Asquith used a documentary style presentation in order to put the events of the war into a real context and perspective. In doing this he gave a preview of what would become England's unique contribution to movie making during World War II. Asquith is one of the important names in British film making. His *Dance, Pretty Lady* (1932), *Pygmalion* (1938), *The Way to the Stars* (1945) and *The Browning Version* (1951) have met with success wherever they have been shown.

As the British industry became more confident, it decided to meet America head-on in the production of lavish spectacles. Alexander Korda is substantially responsible for beginning this movement with his popular *The Private Life of Henry VIII* (1933). Other important films in this cycle were: Victor Saville's *The Good Companions* (1933), Paul Czinner's *Catherine the Great* (1934), Korda's *The Private Life of Don Juan* (1934) and *Rembrandt* (1936) and William K. Howard's *Fire Over England* (1937).

The film Quota Act devised in the late twenties no longer served the betterment of British film makers; so in 1938 a new Quota Act was passed. An important result of the new act was to attract foreign investors. The idea was to employ British and foreign producers and actors in the film. Foreigners would donate money and talent in return for special protections guaranteed by the Quota Act. M.G.M. joined in this venture to produce *A Yank at Oxford* (1938), *The Citadel* (1939) and *Goodbye Mr. Chips* (1939).

World War II: America

World War II again placed Hollywood in the dominant position of film producer to the world. During this period the businessmen connected with movie making experienced their finest hour. Vast numbers of persons with money and time on their hands looked to Hollywood to fill their need for entertainment. Almost every movie produced during this period made money; so again the cry went up around the studios to "crank 'em out faster". A brief glance at the standard bill of fare now offered on late TV movies is enough to discover how desperate for diversion a people can become.

Some movies produced during this period, however, have been able to weather the passage of time. In 1941 Orson Welles produced his remarkable *Citizen Kane*. Competition was given to Welles that year by John Ford's *How Green Was My Valley*, Howard Hawks' *Sergeant York*, John Huston's *The Maltese Falcon* and William Wyler's *The Little Foxes*.

Naturally Hollywood produced several movies dealing with the war. Hollywood paid its respects to British fortitude in William Wyler's *Mrs. Miniver* (1942), and the "hard shell-soft center" Bogart was off to Africa to straighten up the mess there in the Michael Curtiz production, *Casablanca* (1942).

Orson Welles' *The Magnificent Ambersons* (1942), William Wellman's *The Ox-bow Incident* (1943) and Herman Shumlin's *Watch on the Rhine* (1943) are some better productions during the middle war years.

1944 saw the production of several better than average suspense movies. Edward Dymtryck introduced Richard Powell in a complete change of pace from his previous romantic characterizations in *Murder My Sweet*; Otto Preminger produced his classic, *Laura*; Fritz Lang directed Robinson, Bennett and Duryea in *The Woman in the Window* and later *Scarlet Street*; and Billy Wilder presented his sardonic *Double Indemnity*. Yet, it was Leo McCarey and Bing Crosby who pleased the greatest numbers by their sentimental *Going My Way.*

Hollywood did not treat the subject of men in war with anything but soap opera melodrama until the end of the war. In 1945 William Wellman's *The Story of G.I. Joe* and Lewis Milestone's *A Walk in the Sun* at last gave the audience at home a glimpse of the lives of men who had fought and had died on the far away battlefields.

World War II: Europe

Important as Hollywood was during the war, America was by no means the only country producing movies. England, for example, produced some of her best movies during the war years. Such pictures as *Next of Kin* (1942), *In Which We Serve* (1942), *The Way Ahead* (1943), *Henry V* (1944) and *The Way to the Stars* (1945) were valuable morale builders for the British people and did much to further the prestige of British movie making abroad.

Russia too used the film as means to keep up morale during the dark days of the war. While they are propagandistic, still their artistic merit makes them worth seeing today. Examples of Russian war films still available today are: *The Rainbow* (1943), *Girl 217* (1944) and *Ukraine in Flames* (1943). The production of Eisenstein's *Ivan the Terrible* parts I and II (1944 and 1946) belong to this period of Soviet film making, yet their outstanding quality transcends the other pictures of the time.

While movies were made in France during the German occupation, the emigration of several top directors and the refusal of those who remained to make pictures that would serve Nazi aims caused serious restrictions on the quality and subject matter. To a large extent the films dealt with fantasy and bygone days. A good example of this is found in Marcel Carne's *Les Enfants du Paradis* (1944).

Post World War II

Motion picture production has undergone radical reorientation since the end of the war. As television becomes more of a way of life in the countries of the world, vast audiences that were wont to spend their time in movie theaters are now deserting the box office. So far the attempts by movie producers throughout the world to stem this tide away from the theaters have not proved successful. New technical devices like the wide screen, stereophonic sound and lavish technicolor spectacles beyond the power of television have not proved the answer. Although there remains a sufficient audience to still make the typical "Hollywood confection" profitable, the definite pattern of movie attendance shows audiences becoming much more selective. The growing group of discriminating moviegoers has made possible the production and importation of more mature and thought provoking pictures.

A glance at the cinema page in daily newspapers and weekly news magazines shows moviegoing has taken on a distinctly international flavor. Countries like Japan and India, once virtually unknown to Western moviegoers, have become important contributors to the body of world cinema. The movies of Satyajit Ray [*The Apu trilogy* (1957-59), *Two Daughters* (1961), *The Living Room* (1962)], Akira Kurosawa [*Drunken Angel* (1948), *The Men Who Tread on the Tiger's Tail* (1945), *Rashomon* (1950), *The Magnificent Seven* (1954), *Ikuru* (1952), *I Live in Fear* (1955), *Throne of Blood* (1957)], Kon Ichikawa [*The Burmese Harp* (1956)] and Kenji Mizoguchi [*Women of the Night* (1948), *Sancho the Bailiff*

(1954)] are eagerly awaited events by many movie-goers in America.

The Italian film underwent its renascence immediately after the war with films of Rosellini [*Open City* (1945), *Paisan* (1946)], De Sica [*Shoeshine* (1946), *The Bicycle Thief* (1949), *Miracle in Milan* (1951] and Zampa [*To Live in Peace* (1946)]. These so-called "neorealistic" pictures were characterized by stark, documentary-like treatment of postwar suffering. It was not long, however, before sex and violence, once an integral part of the subject matter, began to be used for its own sake in order to capture the American dollar. The quality of Italian movie making began to slump as the "spear and sandal" period was instituted to give competition to the Hollywood spectacle. Attempts to recapture the spirit of "neorealism" in De Sica's *Il Tetto* (1956) and in Rosellini's *Il General Della Rovere* (1958) have not proved too successful because of the use of sets to re-create the war and postwar period.

While Italian studios continue to turn out spectacles and sex farces, the attention of serious moviegoers has been attracted to the work of Frederico Fellini [*La Strada* (1954), *The White Shiek* (1953), *Il Bidone* (1955), *Nights of Cabiria* (1957), *La Dolce Vita* (1960), *8½* (1962)], Michaelangelo Antonioni [*Il Grido* (1958), *L'Avventura* (1960), *La Notte* (1961), *L'Eclipse* (1962)], Luchino Visconti [*Rocco and His Brothers* (1960), *The Leopard* (1963)], Pietro Germi [*Divorce Italian Style* (1963)], and Ermanno Olmi [*The Fiancés* (1963), *The Sound of Trumpets* (1962].

For most moviegoers today, the Swedish film industry is synonymous with the name of Ingmar Bergman. His approach to the subjects of woman [*Illicit Interlude* (1951), *Secrets of Women* (1952), *A Lesson in Love* (1954), *Smiles of a Summer Night* (1955), *Dreams of Women* (1955), *Brink of Life* (1958)] and of God [*The Naked Night* (1953), *The Seventh Seal* (1956), *Wild Strawberries* (1957), *The Magician* (1958), *The Virgin Spring* (1959), *Through a Glass Darkly* (1961), *Winter Light* (1962)], display the talent of a true cinema artist. Bergman has a great deal to say; however, considerable activity on the part of the audience is required to fully appreciate him.

Through the cultural exchange program between the United States and Russia, American moviegoers have a chance to see the work going on within the Soviet Union today. Such films as *Ballad of a Soldier* (1959), *The Cranes Are Flying* (1959), *A Summer to Remember* (1960), *A Lady and Her Dog* (1960) and *My Name is Ivan* (1962) give evidence that creative film making is still possible in Russia.

The film industry in France is composed of two strong forces of film makers. Established prewar directors—Renoir, Clement, Duvivier, Carne, and Clair —continue to produce pictures starring well-known names of the French screen—Gabin, Fernandel, Darrieux, and Signoret—that carry on the prewar traditions of comedy and melodrama. A postwar group of film makers—François Truffaut [*400 Blows* (1959), *Jules and Jim* (1962), *Shoot the Piano Player* (1962)], Jean-Luc Goddard [*Breathless* (1959), *To Live My Life* (1962), *The Little Soldier* (1963)], Claude Chabrol [*The Cousins* (1959)], Alaine Resnais [*Hiroshima Mon Amour* (1959), *Last Year at Marienbad* (1961), *Muriel* (1963)], Louis Malle [*The Lovers* (1960), *Zazie* (1962)], Roger Vadim [*And God Created Women* (1958), *Liaisons Dangereuses* (1962)], Agnes Varda [*Cleo from 5 to 7* (1962)] and Philippe de Broca [*The Love Game* (1960)]—have brought new faces to the screen: Brigitte Bardot, Jeanne Moreau, Jean-Paul Belmondo, Jean-Claude Brialy, and Jean-Pierre Cassel. Nicknamed "the new wave" of French movie making, their films display a youthful and imaginative approach to the problems of young persons afloat in a world not of their making and totally unacceptable to them. In an attempt to find meaning for their lives, they drift from experience to experience often giving way to emotional and physical excesses. While these directors lack a sense of direction in thematic development, still their concern for the problems of human communication gives their films a vitality and urgency often lacking in the productions of more traditional film makers.

Each passing year presents new film makers who are eager to experiment with new techniques and subjects. In America John Cassavettes [*Shadows* (1960)], Frank Perry [*David and Lisa* (1962)], Adolfas Mekas [*Halleluja the Hills* (1963)], and Shirley Clarke [*The Connection* (1962)] are moving away from the traditional Hollywood approach to film making. England too, with her "angry young men" movement, has broken traditional thematic patterns. Writers like John Osborne, Alan Sillitoe, Shelagh Delaney and Stan Barstow have been translated by directors Tony Richardson, Karel Reise and John Schlesinger into strong cinema propaganda on behalf of a new generation of Englishmen. *Look Back in Anger* (1959), *The Entertainer* (1960), *Saturday Night and Sunday Morning* (1961), *A Taste of Honey* (1962), *A Kind of Loving* (1962) and *The Loneliness of the Long Distance Runner* (1962) display the younger generation's attitude toward the Establishment. Lindsay Anderson's *This Sporting Life* (1962) indicates a possible new trend in the "angry" approach in that he seems to be as interested in how he presents something as in what he is presenting.

Of the Iron Curtain countries, Poland appears to have the greatest freedom for expressing itself cinematically. Andrzej Wajada's *Ashes and Diamonds* (1959) and *Kanal* (1960) and Romaine Polanski's *The*

Knife in the Water (1962) have captured the attention and interest of Western audiences.

Manifestly, a great deal more could and should be said about the development of motion pictures. This brief survey, however, was intended to help the beginner orient himself and the films he selects within a historical context. By no means do the authors consider this sketchy treatment to be a substitute for the necessary reading in film history that a serious film student must do.

II

The Language of
the Film

There is a basic analogy or comparison in the back of the minds of those people who refer to film techniques as the *language* of the film. Ernst Cassirer has described man as a symbol-using animal, distinguished from the rest of the animal world not only by his power of intelligence but also by his ability to use symbols to communicate his thoughts. Spoken language was undoubtedly the first development in man's search for self-expression, but since the invention of the alphabet over 4,000 years ago, man has continued to design various systems of signs and symbols to convey his thoughts and feelings to his fellow men.

Art has been one of the great means for man to express through sensible forms his deepest feelings and most profound intuitions. The film art is the most recent of man's endeavors to find an outlet for his inner visions. Like other systems of symbols that man has devised, of which verbal language is certainly the prototype, the film shares with them the basic aim of communication. With this fundamental principle in mind, critics and teachers have striven to show that this art, like its older companion arts, has basic comprehensible principles and an orderly way of approaching a subject. The real necessity is that audiences learn to *see* what the film maker has given them and not remain satisfied with superficial understanding.

Since its beginning in the last decade of the nineteenth century, the motion picture medium has been a language, a system of sensible symbols. It did not emerge fully developed from the laboratories of Edison or Marey but, as the history of the medium shows, only gradually evolved and became refined as men continued to experiment. It remains today a growing medium whose outer limits have not been reached and consequently one for which no final chapter can yet be written. The study of this language of images, however, will help men to read what has thus far been produced.

For the purpose of clarity, one may draw out the comparison between verbal language and film language a bit more. First, a descriptive definition of this particular kind of language may be offered: film language is an organized body of images, ordered in such a way that it communicates the ideas and feelings of the film maker to the audience. This language, like its analogue of verbal language, has a grammar and syntax consisting of the basic components of film technique. To go further, one might also speak of the rhetoric of film making in referring to more complex interrelationships that the editing process generally includes. Finally, style, in this language as in others, is the expression of the personality of the film maker in the medium of the image. It will show itself in the particular ways in which each film maker uses the common techniques of the medium to express his own vision of life.

It is the fantasy of the very young that before they have entered the formal training of school they know their native tongue. Much to the chagrin of the youngster, he must face at least twelve years of exacting training in his own language before he has reached the level of minimum competence in his society. In much the same way, the average audience that has grown up with movies and television feels somewhat put upon when it is told that it does not really understand a language that it has been living with for years. The resistance is often too great to persuade the reluctant adults to go back to school. There are, happily, individuals among the mass audience who are not satisfied with a preschool knowledge of film language. It is for these that this chapter is written.

One can study the complexities of film from many points of view. In the approach to film language in this book, an emphasis will be placed on basic techniques of the medium for two reasons: first, because this is a handbook for those who have not had a great deal of previous training in the analysis of film language; and secondly, because a thorough understanding of the grammar and rhetoric of the medium is absolutely essential for understanding and appreciating the style of a film maker. Since a study of film style would necessitate an analysis of a number of individual directors, such a study is beyond the scope of this brief book. Much has already been written on the styles of the great figures of the film medium, and those interested are urged to read the books and articles that deal exclusively with men like Griffith, Flaherty, Eisenstein, Clair, Pabst, Bergman or Antonioni. This chapter only proposes to set forth those basic techniques that all these men have employed to achieve their success.

Grammar

A film is made up, in its most elementary form, of thousands of individual pictures, each containing within the four sides of its perimeter a whole complex organization of light and shade, line, space and volume; all the elements of visual structure and beauty of the still photograph. These individual pieces are projected onto a screen in such rapid succession that they create the illusion of motion, thus adding one of the unique factors of the film art, the visual image in motion.

It should be noted at the start that the following explanations of various film techniques are not definitions to be memorized but descriptions to be applied to the analysis of a film. Since it is difficult to know what films the readers have seen, examples in the text will be taken, for the most part, from film classics, especially Welles' *Citizen Kane* (1941),[1] and from a few films of more recent vintage that are of more than average merit.

One further practical note should be added. The film society leader cannot expect all members of his group to read this book in detail. He should, therefore, try to pass on his understanding of what is here dealt with in the form of program notes or a synopsis of some point of film language that may pertain to a film on his program. The understanding of film language should always be directed toward the concrete appreciation of a film and should, above all, be a practical means of analysis.

Visual Parts of Speech

Technically a film could be called the sum total of its visual parts. The "word" with which film language is composed, the smallest unit in this world of film, is called a *shot*. It is the basic film unit, taken in one uninterrupted photographic process of the motion picture camera. It is difficult to generalize on the average length of a shot, but someone has estimated that ordinarily shots do not last much longer than twenty or thirty seconds. One immediately begins to think of exceptions like the eight minute marathon at

---

[1] It is presumed that most readers have seen this film at least once.

the opening of Lumet's *Twelve Angry Men* (1957).
On the other hand, there are many examples of shots
that are only a second or two in length as one finds in
Eisenstein's *Potemkin* (1925) or Renais' *Last Year at
Marienbad* (1961). No matter what its length, the
shot is the fundamental unit on which all of the rest
of film language is based.

The next larger unit of a film is called the *scene*.
It consists of a series of shots taken in the same location and during the same brief period of time but
generally from several different angles and camera
placements. The whole series of shots, at the beginning of *Citizen Kane*, for example, formed the opening scene of the film. In this series of shots only one
word is spoken, and yet the variety of shots within the
scene not only created an atmosphere of mystery but
made the audience ask the question: "Who is this
man?"

A number of scenes taken together to form the largest working unit in a film is called a *sequence*. This
is a scriptwriter's term, for the final draft of a film
script is divided into shot, scene, and sequence. Such
divisions roughly approximate the division of a drama
into speech, scene and act. In *Kane* one finds a number of sequences or larger units. The various flashbacks in the film provide rather obvious units; for
example, Jedadiah's memories of Kane or Bernstein's
story. Susan Alexander recalls all the horrors of being made into an opera star in a number of scenes,
culminating in her attempted suicide, all of which may
be called the "Opera Sequence".

Every film contains all three units described above,
the shot, scene and sequence, just as a novel contains
the units of verbal language, the word, sentence and
paragraph. These units are not independent but related to each other by techniques of transition and
continuity.

(a) *Transition:* As in the medium of writing, so in films, there are certain ways of indicating a qualification of a writer's words and the transition of his thought: the exclamation point, question mark, quotations, italics, periods and so forth. In the film medium there are techniques of transition from one shot or scene to another that also qualify the telling of the story. These techniques are the means that the director or editor uses to insure the continuity of his story and carry the audience over easily from one shot to another.

First in importance is the *simple cut* made by joining the frames of different shots to one another. The end of one shot is attached directly to the beginning of another one by means of a photographic adhesive. This simple juxtaposition has the effect of instantaneous change from one image to another and is most commonly used when there is no need for preparing the audience for the transition. When, for example, two people are talking together, the camera will first focus on one person then on the other as the dialogue goes back and forth. This action is usually accomplished by simple cuts and it needs no explanation to the audience. The simple cut can also have the effect of an abrupt transition that may be used to shock the audience. It is even sometimes employed to deliberately confuse the audience, as a way of denying the meaningfulness of temporal sequence or logic in a story as, for example, in Renais' *Last Year at Marienbad* or even in Godard's *Breathless* (1959).

As an audience becomes more sophisticated in its viewing habits, films can make more demands on its ability to follow complex time sequences and instantaneous flashbacks joined together by simple cuts. One finds this abrupt juxtaposition of present and past time by means of the cut in an increasing number of films; for instance, in 1963, there was *My Name Is*

Ivan, The Condemned of Altona and *This Sporting Life.*

The *fade* is another means of transition or continuity. In this technique the shot gradually darkens until the screen is black (*fade-out*) and then slowly lightens (*fade-in*) on a new shot or scene. This kind of transition will usually mark the end of a scene or sequence; it may introduce either a change of place or time. Often it is coupled with some other indication in the scene that time has passed. For example, at the beginning of the fade-out a person is seen sitting in a chair waiting for someone late at night; at the fade-in the same person is asleep in the chair with the sun coming through the window to indicate the passage of night. The fade-out, or black-out, marks a deliberate stop in the flow of images across the screen and should, therefore, be psychologically justified for the place where it occurs in the film. Sometimes there may be only a few fade-outs in a film because there are few places where the story does not flow continuously or else the director has decided that in his film there should be no break in the continuity of his images.

Since the techniques of transition are not part of the original filming process, the editor or director may decide after the film has been shot what kind of transition will best suit the story that is being told. A film like *David and Lisa* (1962), for instance, whose structure consists of a series of brief vignettes showing the development of the relationship between two psychologically disturbed young people, has to be careful not to punctuate the film with too many fade-outs. Otherwise these interruptions might become a major distraction to the audience. A slow fade-out at the close of a film is the most common form of ending and is generally well suited to the situation. In the final minutes, the film's impact on its audience should be at its greatest. The gradual final fade allows time for the audience to come back to reality. This is much the same psychology that is behind the slow curtain and gradual raising of the house lights after a play.

The *dissolve* consists in the superimposition of a fade-out and a fade-in so that there is never complete darkness on the screen but only a blurring of one image and the clarifying of another. This kind of transition is less definitive than the complete fade and so is suitable for change of scene or sequence where the editor or director does not want a complete break in the story continuity. This method, like the complete fade, may represent a passage of time or a psychological shift like a flashback.

There is a closely related technique called the *superimposition* in which the first image is deliberately held so that the two images appear on the screen at the same time. In this way the film maker may indicate to the audience that this is not a mere breaking point but that the two images are somehow linked together in the story. In *Kane*, for instance, there are several examples of the superimposition. At the beginning and the end of the film, there are several shots of Kane's estate carefully linked to one another by the use of superimposition. The director also introduces the reminiscences of Jed Leland by gradual superimposition of the image of Kane's breakfast room in the upper right of the screen while Jed is still seen sitting in his hospital chair at the lower left. The superimposition tells the audience, in perhaps too obvious a way, that this is a memory and a description of Kane from the point of view of his former friend, Leland.

Finally, the *wipe* is a kind of transition in which a line running across the screen replaces one picture with another by seeming to wipe the first away so that the one "beneath" can become visible—a popular form of transition in the silent era, it has never been completely abandoned, though today it is quite rare. One occasionally finds it in contemporary films. For example, Kurosawa's *Ikiru* (1952) uses the wipe with great frequency without harming the effect of the film even for audiences that are unused to it. There are times, too, when a quick wipe from some unexpected angle can add an extra element of surprise and fun to a comic sequence. At this point of film history, however, the wipe remains more an antique than a tool for the movie maker.

(b) *The Seeing Eye of the Camera:* In a film there is only one way of seeing things: through the eye of the camera. The film director has his audience much more under his control than does the stage director because if the audience agrees to watch his film they must watch it on his terms, as he sees it through his mechanical eye. There are no distractions, no danger of dividing one's attention with something else on stage. The camera focuses attention on the object that the director chooses and in the way that he chooses. It seems obvious that the camera as an inert machine cannot make its own comments on the subject matter; but under the control of the director it can become a means of personal comment and represents a definite point of view by its position, angle, movement and even focus.

The static position of the camera in its relation to the subject being photographed will affect the way the audience sees the picture. At the beginning of its historical development, the motion picture camera was in a fixed, eye-level position like its predecessor, the still camera. This position automatically set up a distance relationship with its subject that had important consequences on the finished product. For a few years, most audiences witnessed films from about the fifth row middle of a make-believe stage audience. Today the variety of static camera placements give the director greater freedom to tell his story. These static positions employed in modern film making may be reduced to four main ones: the extreme long shot, the long shot, the medium shot and the close-up.

First in the order of camera positions is the *extreme long shot* which gives the spectator a view of the entire environment and may range in distance from perhaps fifty yards to several miles. At the beginning of certain films, for instance, one often sees an extreme long shot of the Manhattan skyline from a plane circling the city. The director may be trying to establish the location of his story, as in *West Side Story* (1961), or may just need a cliché to get his picture moving. In films where the environment plays an important part in the narrative, as in *Lawrence of Arabia* (1962) or in many westerns, the extreme long shot becomes more than a way of introducing the story; it will be used again and again throughout the film to give expression to the surroundings.

The difference between the extreme long shot and the *long shot* may only be a matter of emphasis, but the latter is described as one ranging from fifty yards to about twenty feet. The long shot can focus on the environment and, at the same time, allow some details of the characters to be observed. It is sometimes called the *establishing shot* because it establishes the visual relationship of the characters with their physical surroundings. For example, in a long shot from overhead showing a group of longshoremen standing around waiting to be hired in Kazan's *On the Waterfront* (1954), one can distinguish the main character of Terry Maloy and yet take in the other workers and the immediate dock area as well.

The *medium shot* focuses on one or two individuals at close enough range to establish clearly the identity of the persons and still include a part of the immediate environment. This is, perhaps, the most com-

mon range for narrative action in the development
of a film. It is a range at which the person may speak
or act with greatest freedom without losing personal
contact, as in a long shot, and without being drawn
into too intimate involvement, as in a close-up. The
medium shot with its great flexibility is a most valuable means for the director to carry on the story action. The shots of Kane and Emily, for instance, in
Welles' famous breakfast room scene in *Kane* are
something between close-ups and medium shots (the
figures are seen from waist up in their immediate
surroundings). The camera is at close enough range
to clearly identify the personal feelings of each, yet
objective enough to allow the director to create a narrative montage that covered a period of years in a
few minutes.

The close-up and the *large close-up* are only academic distinctions that will not mean much until one
sees the two in the concrete. The large close-up or
detail shot of a hand or a mouth has quite a different
purpose and effect from the close-up of the whole face
of a person who registers an emotional reaction in
eyes, mouth and facial muscles. One might contrast
the detail shot of Kane's mouth at the beginning of
Welles' film with the series of close-ups of Kane and
Susan Alexander during the evening of their first
meeting. The first is a technique to point out and
give emphasis to a word in which the audience is not
particularly involved as yet, while the second is a
powerful means of communicating the personal feelings
of the characters with which the audience will em-
pathize.

The close-up as a means of capturing subtle human
emotions and helping the audience to identify with a
character has been overused by television. The human face is the focal point of the external identity of
the person; it is the most personal part of an indi-

vidual and not something that should be carelessly exposed to close scrutiny by an audience. It becomes cheapened when audiences are made to stare at the faces of actors and actresses at close range for long periods unless the director and actors are quite skillful. As an experiment, one might try comparing the use of close-ups in the average dramatic television program and the use of the same technique in a film by Satyajit Ray, for example. One would discover that although the same technique is used quite frequently in both, the effect of the close-up on television is often boring and embarrassing, while Ray's study of faces adds depth and reality to his story.

(c) *Camera Angle:* All that has been said up to now dealt with the position of the camera in relation to the subject. The camera, however, may be focused on the subject from various angles that also affect the shot. In its static position the camera has three common possibilities for angle: *eye-level* or horizontal, *tilt-up* and *tilt-down*. The latter two are obviously taken by the camera at an upward or downward angle.

These two basic angles, up and down, have no universally valid meaning in themselves, though the angle of the camera will have aesthetic and psychological significance when it is seen in the context of its story. It seems clear that Welles in *Kane* wanted to show Kane's domination of Susan in the early part of their marriage, when, on the morning after the opera premiere in Chicago, the two are in the hotel room together reading the notices. Susan is seated on the floor surrounded by clippings and Kane stands over her and tells her to keep quiet. Kane moves closer and his shadow envelops Susan's face. As the camera looks down on Susan, one immediately feels she is in an inferior position. Angle was perhaps enough here; the shadow helped to underline the point. Later in the story, Susan is again at Kane's feet in a tent in the Everglades. He strikes Susan to keep her quiet. The camera again looks down at Susan, then up at Kane towering over her. Now, however, the situation has changed and psychologically it is Susan who, despite the angle of the camera, is in a dominant position. The conclusion is that camera angle speaks only for the context in which it is found.

There is another possibility, not often employed, with regard to camera angle. For the lack of a better term, one might call it *frame-slant*. In this shot, the camera is slightly tilted on its side so that the image will show up on the screen in a tilted, off-balance position. This technique is rarely used because of the danger that it will call attention to itself and distract from the story. In *East of Eden* (1955), for example, Elia Kazan used this angle on several occasions to indicate the disturbed, off-balance relationship that existed between James Dean and his father. In this case it was not successful, for it did call attention to itself, instead of making the audience more aware of the inner conflict of the hero.

(d) *The Mobile Camera:* The mobile camera is an important means of creating the illusion of motion in films. In this case the subject being filmed may be moving or not, but the camera itself moves in a variety of ways that may ultimately be reduced to two: though the camera remains stationary, it pivots on its axis in movements that are called *tilting* and *panning*; the camera actually moves backward, forward, sideways, up or down.

The two pivotal movements of which the camera is capable were introduced rather early in film making and were called the tilt and the pan shots. The first consists in the tilting movement of the camera up or down on its axis while the shot is being taken. This movement is used, for example, when the camera is following the line of a person's eye as he looks up or down. If a small shoeshine boy is working on a customer's shoes, he may slowly look up to see the face of the man standing over him. The camera would imitate this action with a gradual tilt-up shot from the boy's position. The pan shot is made by pivoting the camera around on the same horizontal plane from right to left or left to right. Taken from the word "panoramic", this shot generally indicates that the subject cannot be gotten into one shot from a fixed angle or that the camera is following a continuous action of the subect as he moves from place to place. The pan shot, for example, might be used in a western when the marshal comes into a bar and surveys the men at the tables. The camera pans slowly around the room, simulating the marshal's glance.

It is unclear as to who first actually loosened the camera from its early fixed position; but it is certain that the German team of Murnau, Mayer and Freund, working on *The Last Laugh* (1924), first made extensive use of the camera in long uninterrupted shots where it actually explored the set by moving from place to place. Such mobility added a new flexibility to storytelling and a dimension of reality hitherto unknown to film making. The camera created for the audience of *The Last Laugh* a close identity with the actor Emil Jannings as it followed him around and saw things as he saw them. The mobility of the camera was temporarily halted with the coming of sound several years later. But once it had been freed from its fixed position even sound could not long halt its movements.

The simplest of the shots where the whole camera moves is called a *dolly shot* because the camera was originally attached to a dolly or some kind of wheeled platform. There are stories that in the early years of film making inventive cameramen even used their wives' baby buggies to dolly for shots. Whatever the means used, the purpose was to make the movement of the camera and its resulting shot as smooth and flexible as possible. The camera in *Kane*, for example, makes considerable use of dolly shots with the result that even when there is little or no movement by the actors, one gets the impression of motion from the camera. In the reporter's interview of Bernstein, the two men are first seen in a long shot. The camera gradually moves in on Bernstein until at the time of the flashback, it is in a close-up position of Kane's old business manager. The director could have gone from long shot to medium shot to close-up by means of cutting from one stationary position to another. He decided instead to dolly in one continuous movement from the long shot position to the close-up. The moving shot gave greater fluidity to the scene and allowed no break in the audience's attention to the actor's words.

When action must be followed, paralleled or preceded by the camera for a long distance or over rough terrain, there are several methods for transporting the camera, and the shots are variously called *tracking, trucking* or *traveling* shots. The origin of the terms is obvious enough from the means of transport used or the description of the movement of traveling. When a long moving shot over rough ground is called for by the script, a small track is laid down on which a trolley with a camera and cameraman may be placed to follow the action. One may recall the vivid sense of movement that Kurosawa created in his long tracking shots of the woodcutter walking through the forest in *Rashomon*. When streets or a road are available, an automobile or truck seem best for the job. This is the method most often employed in the western where the hero chases the cattle rustlers over the wide open spaces. There are other means of transport like airplanes and especially helicopters, whose ability to capture certain kinds of action makes their use important to film makers.

There is a final general category of camera motion in which are included the *boom* or *crane shot* and the *zoom shot*. The crane or boom shot is named for the special crane that can lift the camera and crew quickly and smoothly into the air and allow them to look down on the subject from a variety of overhead positions. The zoom shot is simply a matter of lens adjustment that brings one into a rapid close-up view of the subject.

The basic visual grammar of the film, then, is quite simple. It stems from the various relationships of distance, position and movement between the camera and the subject. The visual language of the film is composed of the series of frames in the shot, the scene and the sequence. Each shot, however, is modified according to the camera's position, angle and movement. There is an almost endless possibility of variety with this visual syntax, but in each motion picture it will depend on the creative ability of the film maker to choose the precise way to combine all of these techniques into an artistic whole, stamped with his own personal vision.

Aural Parts of Speech

The Jazz Singer (1927) is frequently cited as the picture that brought sound to the movies. As a matter of fact, sound, in the form of some kind of musical accompaniment, had been a feature of films from their earliest commercial exploitation. The silent visual image has rarely been enough to carry audience interest except at short intervals during the film. Sound is not the dominant element in a film whose main component is, as has been stated, the moving image. But neither is sound a mere accidental, whose presence or absence is irrelevant to the medium. So much do accompanying sounds add to the perception of the visual image itself that the human voice, natural noises and music are essential elements of film language that help to create the full reality of any feature film.

(a) *Voice:* The most common kind of sound in films today is the human voice in dialogue. The voices of the actors are synchronized on the sound track with the images of them speaking to create the illusion of hearing real people in conversation. Dialogue is as much a necessity at times as the shots themselves, for the voice is man's most common means of expressing his thoughts and feelings. Since the beginning of sound there have been few feature films that have gotten along without a minimum of dialogue or narration. By way of exception, one may recall Kaneto Shindo's *The Island* (1962), as a recent example of a film that used practically no sound of any kind to tell its story. But this is only one film in contrast to many hundreds that use dialogue to develop their plots.

The criterion of good dialogue is that it expresses what is necessary to the situation and does not repeat what the visual image has already shown. The greatest fault in the combination of image and dialogue is the redundancy of the two elements in telling the story. If the shot shows a girl crying, there is no need to have the girl say how sad she is. If the dialogue can make the same point, there is no need to tell the audience the same thing by showing her in tears. It would be much better in the latter case to show the girl's father and his reaction to the situation.

The human voice may come from a source off-screen. This is called *commentative sound* or the *commentative voice*. It is often found in the teaching or documentary film where, for example, the audience might be shown a glass blower at work and have the art explained by the voice of an unseen observer. The use of the similar technique of the narrator in a feature film is infrequent but may be used, for instance, to indicate childhood recollections or the entry in a diary as in *To Kill a Mockingbird* (1963) and *Diary of a Country Priest* (1951).

(b) *Natural Sound:* Besides the human voice there are many other sounds from the environment that help convey meaning. These sound sources in films are more commonly realistic, that is, they come from the objects pictured or implied to exist in the world of the film. They may also be symbolic, that is, the objects on the screen are given a heightened meaning by associating them with sounds from a completely different source. Realistic sound is far more common in films: the roaring of the crowd at a game as in *This Sporting Life* or at a fight as in *Champion* (1949) or *The Set-Up* (1949); the slam of a car door, traffic noises, bells, dogs barking or children playing.

There are occasions when the film maker can improve his story by using a sound metaphor which suggests rather than tells what it means in a straightforward, realistic manner. Like a verbal metaphor, the sound metaphor can be used to heighten the meaning of the visual image. Such a symbolic use of sound may be found in *Kane* at the end of Susan's opera tour. One sees a backstage warning light fade out and hears a sound like a record grinding to a halt. The next shot is of Susan's bedroom where she has attempted suicide by an overdose of sleeping pills. Welles has given the audience in the first shot a visual and sound metaphor of what has happened in the next shot; Susan can take the pressure no longer and her career fades like the light and the sound. Since it was a career in opera, the sound was especially appropriate.

Completely unrealistic sound can add humor with a caustic edge as René Clair showed in his *Le Million*

(1931) where a scramble for a valuable lottery ticket by a group of supposedly dignified people is shown, while from the sound track come noises of a rugby match in full tilt. In De Sica's *Miracle of Milan* (1952), the argument of two capitalists over a piece of property changes from angry words to the vicious barking of dogs. These are only indications of how sound may be used to support, explain, counterpoint or make light of the image on the screen.

(c) *Music:* What has been said of sound can be applied to film music with suitable qualifications. Good film music is a secondary, supporting factor in the film medium. Generally its function is to provide a background, transition or comment for the visual image. The most successful film music is often that which is most difficult to remember once the film is over because it has been so integrated with the visual elements that it has helped the audience to enjoy the images more completely without drawing attention to itself.

Film music is generally used as background or comment on the narrative. Its purpose is to help the audience more fully exploit the image by providing an emotional resonance that gives the visual image greater opportunity of striking root in the imagination of the viewer. At its best the music in a film can be an interpretative or guiding factor for a particular scene. It can also degenerate into an obtrusive element that forces certain stock emotions upon the audience without any effort to evoke them from characters of the film story and its visual images. The more honest but more difficult way is the harmonious combination of image and sound. At the opening of *Kane* the solemn mysterious music is fitted to the slow camera movements and the somber images of Kane's Florida estate. There are cases where the music in a film, though good in itself, is not suited to the situation.

Elia Kazan's *On the Waterfront* has a score by
Leonard Bernstein that seems far too dramatic for
the modest realism of the Hoboken dock area; consequently, it is often out of proportion with the story—
though it must be added that Kazan's somewhat flam-
boyant direction was more in line with the music than
with his realistic story and location.

There is, besides background, interpretative and
bridge music, a category that one might call *incidental
music*: music coming from a realistic sound source
within the film. If a character in the story plays the
piano, whistles or sings, he provides music whose
function will depend upon the circumstances of the
particular story. In the biographies of musicians and
singers, like *Song to Remember* (1945), *Song Without End* (1950) or *Rhapsody in Blue* (1945), music
is an integral part of the narrative because it was so
intimate a part of the person whose story is being told.

There is another common use of music in films
called a *leitmotif*. Its function is to intensify the
emotional response made by the repetition of a melody or musical theme which is identified with a character or set of characters. For example, in *La Strada*
(1954), there is a special melody that is associated
with the heroine Gelsomina. She has learned it from
the Fool and plays it on her trumpet during the scene
at the convent. It is repeated several times during the
last part of the film and comes back with full impact
toward the end of the film when Zampano hears it
being sung by a stranger and finds out from her that
Gelsomina is dead. Another use of the recurring melody or leitmotif is found in Kurosawa's *Ikiru*. At the
beginning of the film, after Mr. Watanabe has discovered that he has an incurable cancer, he goes on
a spree in Tokyo to forget his death sentence. In a
bar he sings a pathetic old love song called "Life is
Short". The melody, at first so melancholy, becomes

a leitmotif for Watanabe who repeats the song later
in the film. At this point the emotional circumstances
have changed because the hero has found some meaning to his life. The repetition helps the audience share
that ambivalent emotion of joy and sorrow that Watanabe feels just before his death. Repetition of a
melody for purposes of irony is found in the English
production of *Romeo and Juliet* (1956). The song
"La Primavera" which was being played at the first
meeting of the lovers at the Capulet ball is repeated
at the end of the film when Juliet discovers the dead
Romeo and decides to join him in death. The beauti-
ful love song of the beginning returns to make an
ironic comment on the waste of the lives of the two
young lovers because of the senseless family feud.

Finally, there is the *musical*. It is a film genre
unlike the film biography of a musician or the film
that uses music for background or bridge purposes.
The music in this kind of film does not have to be
realistically justified as it does in the musical biography because the musical is a form of film fantasy
whose roots are not in the tradition of realism. When
the movies began to talk, they also began to sing.
Many comedies of the early 1930's added song and
dance numbers to the script without worrying much
whether they fitted or not. People were so thrilled
with music and song that the film makers were not
overly concerned about spoiling the unity of their
films. The Marx Brothers, for example, added some
gratuitous routines in a comedy like *A Day at the
Races* (1937). Whether the musical originated in the
studio or came from Broadway, it has been accepted
as a film genre with enormous popularity both here
and abroad. One might call to mind some of the more
popular recent musicals like *On The Town* (1949),
Singin' in the Rain (1952), *The King and I* (1956)
and *West Side Story* (1961).

The sound elements outlined above are techniques that have been developed in an effort to enrich the basic film grammar and give greater range to the film maker to fully communicate his experiences. The visual and aural techniques are the grammar and syntax of a language, and like their visual counterparts, they help men to speak to one another clearly and precisely. These techniques, however, are not enough to account for the power of the film medium to draw an audience into its world. The film maker must not only know the parts of his language but have the skill of ordering all of the elements of his craft into a unified and moving story.

Rhetoric

No man has ever written a piece of literature with only a knowledge of grammar or syntax. The writer must go beyond the stage of mere mechanical correctness and create such an order in telling his story that it will move people in the way that he wants. If the author is Agatha Christie, she will have a certain way of putting her story together so as to create interest and suspense for her readers. Or, if Hemingway wanted dramatic tension in his short story, he did not waste many words on trivial descriptions nor long reflections but concentrated on short sentences and terse dialogue. Each of these authors knew the mechanics of language, to be sure, but what makes them successful writers is the skill with which they have put all of the parts of their stories together.

The editing process in a film may be described as the order and duration of the shots decided upon by the editor or director. This skill of ordering is at the heart of film language, the most difficult and yet most important of the techniques that a film maker must acquire. In the average feature film there are usually four or five hundred separate shots that must somehow be assembled. The order to be imposed, however, is not ordinarily the same as the order in which the film was shot because the scenes following one another are sometimes at great distances from each other and must be taken when weather and other conditions are favorable (for example, when the star actor is free from other commitments). Separate scenes are shot in the order of convenience; then the pieces are spliced together to form a rough draft or rough cut of the film story. It is in this process of assemblage and juxtaposition that the art of the film differs most profoundly from that of writing. Agatha Christie does not write her novels in small pieces, then assemble them with scissors and paste. The writer ordinarily writes through his story as he conceives it, from beginning to end. He may add or delete parts later but this will only be incidental. In film making the pieces of exposed film are the matter on which the creative editor or director works to form the artistic whole. The creative element of the editing process was, perhaps, exaggerated by some of the early Russian film makers.[2] Still, the editing or putting together of the shots and scenes and the determining of their precise order and duration, even for contemporary film makers, remains a crucial factor in the success or failure of a film.

The motion picture is in some ways more closely related to music than to literary art. Time is somehow of the essence of both film and music. There are many aspects of time in a film: the timing of the various

---

[2] For examples of the degree to which editing became the all consuming end of the early Russian films, in theory at least, consult Pudovkin's Chapter "the Plastic Material" in *Film Techniques and Film Acting* or almost any of Eisenstein's early essays in the double edition of *Film Form and the Film Sense.*

movements of subject and camera; the duration of shots to create a rhythm within a scene or sequence; and the time within the story itself that the film maker creates. It is this last aspect that shall be dealt with next.

On its most basic level, a feature film tells a story that must have an order of time, whether it be a straightforward chronological one or one as highly complex and difficult as in Renais' *Last Year at Marienbad*. Most films will follow a chronological order of events, beginning at a given point in time and following straight through to the end of the story. By means of the principle of selectivity, that is always at work in the artistic process, the film maker will show events in such a way that he telescopes the time the story would really take and create a time of his own. This time one might call *narrative* or *story time*, as opposed to *real time* or the *running time* of the film. The power to create another order of time, to give the audience a sense of the flow of actual time in events happening on the screen that may be hours, days or years apart in actual fact, is one of the unique contributions of film. The motion picture can create an illusion of unity and reality in the flow of events that neither the novel nor the drama can rival, though both of these artistic forms must also be highly selective in telling a story.

The film maker has other ways of manipulating narrative time than simply selecting and joining together a number of episodes in chronological order. Instead of moving straightforward in time, the film maker, like the novelist, may hope to achieve a more effective story by returning to the past from a present point in time. This technique, called the *flashback*, has been the common heritage of both the drama and the film literature. A film may use this technique to return temporarily to the past, in order to carry on the main story in the present. A film story may, however, begin with a present event and then spend the major part of the story in the past trying to explain what has just taken place. For example, in the film version of Nabakov's novel *Lolita* (1962), the climactic action of Humbert's story is presented in the first ten minutes of the film when he kills a man named Jay Quilty. The director, Stanley Kubrick, spends the rest of the time explaining the events and motivation that led up to the shooting of Quilty.

The editor can do more than manipulate time through his art of ordering shots; he also can relate several lines of action that may be taking place simultaneously. In the technique of *parallel editing* that D. W. Griffith introduced early in the era of silent film making, the audience did not remain watching one subject in one location for the duration of the action but was presented other events that were related to this action but were happening in a different place. The famous Griffith last minute rescues are the best examples of this process. The hero is pictured on his way to save the heroine who is in the clutches of the villain. The film cuts to the villain who is about to do away with the heroine because she has rejected his advances. The picture cuts back to the approaching hero and continues this process with an increasing tempo so that the audience shares in the excitement and suspense of the rescue. Those who remember the final moments before the gun fight in *High Noon* (1952) recall that Fred Zinnemann used a short period of rapid editing to cap the suspense that the picture had built up.

The particular theory of editing espoused by Eisenstein and Pudovkin is far too complicated to treat in a book of this kind, but one should note that when certain authors refer to *montage* they are speaking of it in the sense in which it was first given theoret-

ical development by Eisenstein and not in a general
sense of the editing process. The principles of the
Russian theorists may be studied in their writings,
especially *Film Form* and *The Film Sense* by Eisenstein and *Film Techniques and Film Acting* by Pudovkin. It would be worth the effort to compare theory
with practice in the films of these two men that are
available.[3] It is worth noting that the creative function of editing that these men so stressed during the
silent era has been, in the contemporary cinema, largely set aside for other techniques that are more in keeping with new ideas and new mechanical factors, such
as the wide screen.

Another important function of timing in films is
the rhythm or pace of the shots. The editor's primary
function is to decide upon the duration of each shot
and to create within each unit a rhythm and flow of
images on the screen. In this work he resembles the
poet who creates a rhythm with the words of his story.
The flow of images should be adjusted to the kind of
story that is being told and the particular quality
of the part of the story that is taking place. Rhythm
and pace are essential to the success of any film but
more so to some kinds than others. In a film poem
where the whole point is to create a rhythm of images,
the editing and exact timing is of capital importance.
In Ruttmann's poetic documentary, *Berlin, the Symphony of a City* (1927), the title itself indicates the
main intent of the film. In a feature length film like
Mizoguchi's *Ugetsu* (1952) or Kurosawa's *Rashomon*
(1950) the rhythm is essential to the overall impression of the tale that is being told. There will, of

---

[3] Consult Appendix C, under directors, for the availability of the films of Pudovkin and Eisenstein. Brandon
Films generally has the largest collection of early Russian films.

course, be entirely different kinds of pace for comedies (like those of Clair or Wilder), serious dramas (Bresson, Antonioni) and adventure thrillers (Hitchcock, Hawks).

The rhythm of the images in most cases will not be noticeable to the audience, though critics who are sensitive to such things will notice the harmony between the mood and theme of the story and the flow of visuals on the screen. A case where the rhythm of the editing is clear even to the most untrained observer is in Eisenstein's Odessa Steps sequence in *Potemkin* (1925). Here the editing is suited to the headlong flight of the crowds and the relentless onslaught of the czarist troops, so much so that the tremendous excitement of this part of the film can be attributed to the editing process almost exclusively. On the other hand, only a few may be conscious of the rhythm of Satyajit Ray's images in his Apu trilogy because they are on the whole leisurely and contemplative; yet there is a definite rhythm at work in the three films and it affects the impression the story of Apu makes upon the audience.

It must be admitted that films like those cited above where the rhythm or pace of the shots are carefully adapted to the peculiar mood of the scenes are rare. It is much more common to find that even in a motion picture that is otherwise well-made the editing seems to have been carried out with little regard to the fine nuance of mood and impression in the story.

Conclusion

One cannot conclude an analysis of film language without adverting to this truism, so obvious in literature, that no amount of knowledge of technique can substitute for the creative ability of the author in fusing the diverse elements of his medium into a unified whole. A well-made film can be as dead as any well-made play. The kind of spirit that quickens technique into art is unique to each creative film maker. Kurosawa can use techniques that are old-fashioned and produce a film that is alive with passion and humanity. Welles could take all of the technique that he learned from watching old movies at RKO and create a *Citizen Kane*. Style is that peculiarity that marks off the film maker from the technician. A few words have been said about style in another section of this book and very little can be added here; for to speak meaningfully of style one must analyze the work of the individual film maker, which is beyond the purpose of this brief chapter. Directors like Bergman, Clair, Mizoguchi, Fellini, Flaherty, Welles, to name but a few, have imprinted their personality on their films. Perhaps because of the nature of the film medium, which involves so many intermediary hands between the conception of the film in the mind of the director and its final accomplishment, there are fewer men of marked style in motion pictures than in the other arts. Style is the precise way in which *this* man uses the techniques of film language to tell his story. If he has been fortunate, all of the elements in his creation are fused in such a way that at least a part of his vision is communicated to the audience. When this fusion happens at its highest level a masterpiece is created.

No one can possibly grasp the full implications of a great work of art at one time. In the art of the film, repeated viewings are necessary. The question is thus raised as to how such viewings are possible. The "art theater" is of some help. The systematic programming of the Museum of Modern Art in New York is a rare opportunity available to a relative few. Renting film for a private showing would be financially prohibitive. The alternative solution is the film study group or society.

III

The Film Society

An interesting paradox of our time is found in the strange pattern of movie attendance since the end of World War II. The great masses who weekly flocked to the local Bijou and the downtown movie palaces have disappeared, satisfied now to sit at home before "the ever-burning eye". This desertion of the once most popular of the "popular arts" has left in its wake darkened theaters, a drastically reduced production schedule at the Hollywood studios, and, ironically, an ever-growing group of persons who take the movies very seriously. Articles in newspapers and magazines proclaim that Hollywood is dying, yet the same newspapers and magazines also carry articles describing the growing attendance at "art theaters". There can be no doubt, except for the occasional blockbuster which "one really owes it to himself to see", the good-old-days of SRO are past; but this is not to say that movie interest is dying out. On the contrary, there is evidence that interest is more intense and articulate than ever before.

In addition to the growth of "art theaters", specializing in international film fare, an ever-increasing number of colleges and universities have instituted film societies on their campuses. Many colleges and high schools now offer courses in motion picture appreciation. Adult study groups, attached to educational institutions and churches, are turning their attention to the movies.

Unfortunately there has been very little written about organizing a film society or film study group.

One finds a great deal of exhortation to form "proper" critical judgment, yet little information is given to show him how he is to go about this operation. Many persons, eager to do something, have banded together to see "the good" movies of past and present. In some cases these groups are very successful; often, however, because they lack leadership and a real sense of direction, they either fail or settle for second best. By second best is meant a group that calls itself a film society, yet is nothing more than a very small-time 16mm commercial theater. Members come and go, satisfied by mere exposure to particular movies, but with no advancement in their appreciation or critical judgments.

This is not to say, however, that the work of commercial "art theaters" and their 16mm counterparts do not have an important part to play in the development of motion pictures. To a large extent, these exhibitors have been responsible for an ever-widening interest in the movies. Were it not for these outlets, many classics of yesterday and vital experiments of today would be lost or might not even see the light of day.

The Role of the Film Society

"Art theaters" and film societies can and do exist side by side in a community and, inasmuch as both strive to bring films of merit to their audiences, they have common aims. When, however, a film society presents itself as a mere replica of an "art theater", it does not live up to its potential and, consequently, fails both its members and the community. In order for a film society to function meaningfully, therefore, a clear distinction must be made between the aims of an "art theater" and a film society. Perhaps the best way to understand this distinction would be to con-

sider the factors leading to a need for both film societies and specialized cinemas.

Since it belongs to the nature of motion picture distribution that a film is here today and gone tomorrow,
often for good, serious filmgoers have long been troubled by difficulties involved in seeing, and re-seeing
certain pictures. Often, except in some large cities,
certain films are never made available to the public at
large because of language or specialized subject matter. To overcome the handicap of short commercial
exposure, to revive classic pictures, and to exhibit
films that were not locally shown motivate the formation of many film societies. Such an enterprise, however, belongs more to the aims of a specialized cinema
than to a film society. The reason for this statement
is basic to the fundamental difference between a commercial theater and a film society. The fundamental
purpose of a commercial theater is to exhibit movies.
A film society goes beyond this purpose of mere exhibition inasmuch as its purpose for existence is to
afford its members opportunities for study and discussion. Very rarely will the beginning student of
cinema develop his critical judgment of movies by
mere exposure.

Development of appreciation and critical judgment
implies a certain amount of organized study. The
fundamental aim of a film society, then, should be to
stimulate discussion and analysis of the pictures it
selects. Since organized discussion is clearly outside
of the province of commercial exhibition, the discussion after a film society's showing should become as
important in the minds of the members as viewing the
picture itself.

Programming of a society's series should be so designed as to make the learning process a profitable
experience for the members. Since there is often little opportunity to see older films in commercial the-

aters, especially is this true in the case of silent movies, a prime function of a film society should be to make these films available for study of their historic and artistic merits. A society would do well to arrange programs which combine old and new films (in that order), thus enabling the members to better understand the development of the motion pictures.

While this distinction between "art theaters" and film societies seems to be logical and necessary, evidence of existing practices in the United States today indicates that no real distinction is made. The results of a survey of film societies, conducted by one of the authors and included in Appendix B, give an indication of the general pattern of activity current today.

A film group located in a small town where no "art theater" is operating will understandably tend to usurp the ends of a commercial theater. Still, to rest satisfied with this function alone is to fall far short of its potential. Mere exposure to an artistic experience will not necessarily result in developing taste or in forming mature criteria for judgment. Most persons are aware of this fact when it comes to developing appreciation and critical judgment of music, art and literature; yet many do not recognize the similar necessity when they approach motion pictures.

For many years, movies have been thought to be merely a source of casual entertainment and diversion. Since this attitude has permeated the mass of American moviegoers, makers of movies, particularly Hollywood, have produced movies that have a minimum of thought content and a maximum of action and emotional stimulation. Although many have been satisfied to maintain critical judgment of movies on the level of "I liked it" or "I didn't like it", there is an evergrowing body of moviegoers who desire to found their judgment upon intellectual norms rather than upon emotional reaction.

Establishing the Society and Clarifying Its Purposes

Once three or four persons have decided that they have the interest and are willing to put in the time and energy required for establishing a film society, their first step will be to consider precisely what strata of their community will form the intended membership of the society. Since art is a co-creative process between the artist and the audience, understanding and appreciation of movies, as with other art forms, is greatly dependent upon the background and maturity of the viewers. Movies say different things to different audiences; so, manifestly, films to be chosen and levels of discussion will vary greatly between high school and college groups and between professional and non-professional men and women.

In the beginning stages of audience recruitment, it will soon become evident that the potential membership of the society will not share the initial enthusiasm of the founders. The organizers, then, will have to use imagination and care in the way the membership campaign is conducted. A certain part of any audience will be composed of persons who join out of curiosity and then move on to some other project. It is important that the membership drive be conducted in such a way as to keep this type of member in the minimum. If the society is to last, care must be employed in attracting a stable core of interested members. To achieve this end the organizers of the society must have clearly in mind the ends they desire for the society and take care that this end is communicated to the potential members.

From the very outset, then, the society founders must decide: do we expect this society to further knowledge and appreciation of movies through planned programming and discussions or do we want to serve as a specialized cinema making available to the members those films not found in the local theaters? If the founders choose to act as a specialized cinema, then the approach to programming and audience attraction will be conducted in much the same manner as that employed by commercial theaters. The membership of this type of society will tend to be quite fluid, interest growing or lessening according to the ability of the society to present attractive film fare.

If, on the other hand, the aim of the society is to be education and appreciation, then the membership drive will be directed toward those persons who are interested in this more serious approach to moviegoing. Membership in this type of society tends to be more stable than the group mentioned above, since interest does not depend solely upon the particular films presented. While it is possible for the specialized cinema society to approach the community at large for its potential members, the film study society should restrict its membership drive to those persons possessing similar educational levels. Profitable study and discussion can be carried on at all levels—high school, college, adult groups—but it is unwise to overlap. Common interests and education are important in developing the co-creative process of film appreciation spoken of above.

Those planning to organize a film society or who are currently involved in such an enterprise will be interested in the more practical aspects of this type of undertaking. However, as the general reader might not have similar interests, we have gathered this information in Appendix A; "Hints on the Organization of a Film Society", p. 134.

Programming

Probably the most difficult task in organizing a film society is programming. Here, you are very much on your own and the success or failure of the project depends upon an ability to select programs so balanced in content and treatment that the aims of a society are met without sacrificing necessary diversity of film selection that will lead to continued interest by the members. If those who compose the program committee lack a feeling for these things, the society will soon wither away.

One need not think, however, that successful programming is impossible. If the aims of the society are made clear when you draw the members together and if you keep always in mind the particular tastes and interests of the members, many of the difficulties of programming will have been overcome at the outset.

The essential factor in good programming is to be found in an ability to tailor film selection to the specific needs of a particular society. To do this you will not only have to know the interests of your members, you will also have to know what films are available. You might be helped in selection by observing the various booking trends of other societies. Appendix B gives a frequency chart for several societies during 1962-1964. Often you will find the titles of film series used in some film societies listed in the Newsletter of the American Federation of Film Societies. Valuable as such lists may be, however, you cannot expect to find a list of films guaranteed to satisfy every group. Even a series of traditional film classics will not automatically assure success if these films do not fulfill the here-and-now needs and interests of a particular group. Imagination and an ability to sound out the feelings of the group will enable you to make the necessary program adjustments.

The presupposition has been that you will select persons for your society who are eager to discuss form and content, historical development and socio-psychological influence found in particular films. For such a group, then, problems of programming resolve themselves to selecting those pictures that will best illustrate the particular point of discussion. So, for example, if a series is devoted to studying the development of the western as a vehicle for social commentary, you will want to begin with Hart, Cruze and Ford of the twenties to taste the beginnings of the western genre. Next you will want to consider the western of the thirties and the use of the individualist hero: Mix, McCoy, and Gibson, and the big budget western of de Mille (*The Plainsman*) and Ford (*Stagecoach*). The forties saw the western dividing itself more radically into low budget entertainments and big budget productions employing actors not primarily connected with the western genre: Ford (*My Darling Clementine*), Hawks (*Red River*) and Wellman (*Yellow Sky*). The fifties and sixties see the western still used as an action vehicle, but there is also the use of the western background to tell stories of more universal importance: Zinnemann (*High Noon*) and Mann (*Hud*).

In Appendix C you will find some suggestions for other film series. These are presented as stimulants to assist your work in preparing programs suitable to your particular group.

A film society composed of members eager to discuss film making and the influence of the film upon contemporary society is still at present an ideal. A survey of the current practices of American film society activity shows these societies to be composed of persons who join a group where "better" films are made available. These persons prefer to have their film understanding develop as a result of their exposure to the movie with the assistance of occasional notes handed out at the showings. The recurrent aim expressed by the officers of these groups, especially is this true in the case of college and university film societies, is to make available to the group those films they would not otherwise be able to see. This means, then, that programs for these groups are made up of pictures that have either completed commercial exhibition or have not been shown in the community at all because of limited commercial appeal of the film.

Membership in this casual type of society tends to be more unstable than that found in a study-type society, since the attitude of the casual member tends to be much like that shown by persons who attend showings at commercial "art" theaters, that is to say, "You pays your money, and you takes your choice". Officers who run this type of society, then, must first of all be businessmen who are skilled in sensing the interests of the masses and are capable of selecting films that will attract the casual filmgoer. The norm generally used for such booking is to follow the reviews found in the popular weekly magazines.

Although the casual film society is more common today, there is evidence of a trend toward the study and discussion film society. As more schools offer classes in motion picture appreciation there is an ever-growing body of persons desirous of continuing their study and appreciation. Also the complexity of many of the films produced today—Bergman's *Wild Strawberries, Magician,* etc.; Renais' *Last Year at Marienbad*; and Fellini's *La Dolce Vita*, $8\frac{1}{2}$—are forcing the audience to question and discuss what they have just seen. For this reason, basic to any understanding of the motion picture is the study of the language of the film.

Teaching Film Language

The film society or that part of the film society that wishes to make a more serious study of film language might make a beginning by setting aside a time to discuss each of the films of the series. If it can be arranged, a second screening of the films should be arranged; it will add depth to the analysis. Before the series begins, however, it would be valuable to introduce the group to some of the basic notions of film language so that each film of the series can be discussed in terms of technique as well as of theme or content.

Since textbooks in English about film language are difficult to find,[4] the group leader might try to summarize the more important ideas of this chapter and mimeograph a page or two for each discussion group member. With a schematic view of the main ideas, people will be able to follow a clear summary presentation of film language in a lecture given by a competent person. If time permits even a second or third lecture, followed by questions and discussion, might be devoted to this topic. In this case, it would be better to have examples of films at hand so that the discussion does not remain in the realm of abstract theory. In the course of the introductory talks, short films or excerpts might be used to illustrate the various elements of film grammar and rhetoric. The British Film Institute has prepared several teaching films that would be helpful for this purpose. Contemporary Films, Inc., controls most of them: for example, excerpts from *Great Expectations, The Overlanders, Odd Man Out, Twelve Angry Men.* If excerpts are to be used, the discussion leader should have previewed the films and decided how he plans to use them in his presentation.

---

[4] The film society leader may wish to consult some of the following sources: Dorothy B. Jones, "The Language of Our Time", an article distributed by Films, Inc.; Edward Fischer, *The Screen Arts*, Ch. 5; Karel Reisz, *The Technique of Film Editing*, a book worth reading in its entirety; Marcel Martin, *Le langage cinématographique* (Paris: 1962), a valuable reference work for those who read French.

Once the group has been introduced to the basic notions of film language, they will be able to use the films of the regular film society series to discuss further problems and questions of technique. It is hoped that this kind of introduction to film analysis will afford the film society or some part of it a greater appreciation and sharper critical judgment.

Better prepared and more carefully analytic program notes will be another means of helping the audience learn the basic elements of film language. Whether the group has been exposed to any kind of formal introduction or not, the film society leader may give his audience a start in this direction by occasionally handing out a summary of one or other key ideas of film language and then commenting briefly on its application to some film that the group has seen.

The aim of the film society is to help the audience grow in its appreciation and knowledge of the film medium. This end will not be accomplished by mere exposure, for the members of the film society must first be taught to read the language of the medium.

Program Notes

The policy of handing out program notes has become standard practice for most film societies operating in the United States today. Source and quality of the notes varies widely from one society to another. Some groups prefer to use notes prepared by someone other than themselves. (Program notes are available from Art Film Publications, Chicago Center for Film Study, Program Note Exchange of the American Federation of Film Societies, and St. Clement's Film Association. [Addresses of these organizations will be found in Appendix A.] Other societies prefer to write their own notes in order to tailor them to the specific needs of their group. For this approach, common source material comes from such standard film histories as *The Film Till Now, From Caligeri to Hitler, Kino: A History of the Russian and Soviet Film,* and *The Japanese Film*; standard film journals such as *Sight and Sound, Film Quarterly, Film Culture*; and from the reviews found in magazines and newspapers. [Complete reference for these books and periodicals will be found in Appendix D.].)

A valuable set of film notes has been published by the Wisconsin Film Society. The technique used in these notes is well worth imitating by any society. The notes are divided into two parts: background information intended to be read before the showing, and analysis of the picture designed to help in the discussion after the showing.

Discussion

To say that the purpose of discussion is to arrive at the meaning of a movie seems almost too obvious; yet much of what calls itself discussion in many film societies is really nothing more than members simply expressing their emotional reactions to a picture in the vague expressions of "I liked it" or "I didn't like it". Such casual opinion exchanging is quite natural in the light of the general attitude Americans have toward motion pictures. Because we have been going to movies for many years, often from an early age, we have tended to develop an attitude that we are fully capable of understanding all that goes on before us and that our reactions to a picture are equally as valid as those of any other person. For the most part, movies originating in Hollywood are of such a nature that this presupposition might well be true. But this is not always the case; when an American or foreign movie treats its subject with skill and depth the standard yardstick of uncultivated opinion is not sufficient for proper understanding, much less competent judgment. Since membership in your society indicates the members are more than casual Saturday night movie-goers, an important function for the society will be to help the members develop a yardstick for total emotional and intellectual understanding.

What, then, are the elements to be considered in establishing such a yardstick? Before these elements are developed, however, it would be wise to consider what force the word *meaning* has when used in the phrase "meaning of a movie".

By *meaning* three points can be understood: (1) the idea of the movie's subject matter itself, (2) the idea behind the film maker's treatment of the subject matter, and (3) the idea of the movie as understood by the audience.

As in all art, the underlying force of a film is found in an idea—the significant idea that the artist wants to transmit to his audience, couched in this or that subject matter and developed in this or that manner. Since motion pictures are made to be seen by many persons in diverse places, the co-creative interchange between audience and film maker needs also to be considered. *Meaning* when applied to a movie, then, is more than an accurate expression of the events and characters; the particular personality of the film maker and the audience synthesis are also vital factors.

When these three points are applied to a picture, immediately there arises a question of point of view. The problem can be expressed as "meaning of a film: for whom?" In your analysis of a movie you will be able to consider four distinct points of view: (1) a person operating as an individual and as a member of a group, (2) the audience operating as a group, (3) the film maker—generally this function is attributed to the director operating as interpreter of a screen writer, and (4) the community at large.

(a) *Individual:* When an individual sees a movie

he is really two persons. First, he is one among many, functioning as a gregarious animal enjoying an experience in concert with others, acting upon and reacting to the total group. His laughter adds to his neighbor's enjoyment. In short, the emotional resonance encountered by the whole group plays an important part in an ultimate appreciation of this artistic experience.

While an individual is part of an audience, still he is a unique person with a complex of personal experiences that cause him to react to the stimuli of an artistic experience in a way different from those around him. Each movie, therefore, speaks to an individual person, affording him the opportunity to make a new affirmation about his outlook on the subject matter as presented. This point of view, then, poses the question: "What meaning has this movie for me?" And the answer is discovered by a person's understanding himself and the influences of his fellow audience.

(b) *Audience:* Another point of view that is important has to do with the ability of a particular here-and-now audience to understand the literal meaning of the movie. In short, does the subject matter of a movie make sense to the spectators? This becomes a real problem when you are using foreign films, since customs, facts of local history, and particular social problems may be of such a nature that they are meaningful only for the country of origin but convey nothing to audiences of differing cultures and experience. This problem should not be thought of only in terms of foreign films. American movies of silent and early sound vintage often contain allusions to matters known to the contemporary audience and, consequently, not requiring explicit development. Today's audience lacking knowledge of certain necessary points of the story will find themselves unable to grasp a total understanding of the picture.

Sometimes, as in other art forms, movies make use of ideas and symbols drawn from our common cultural heritage. The Bible and Graeco-Roman mythology are often used as sources for symbolic connotation. A problem arises, however, when an audience is not adequately acquainted with the symbolic reference. *Sundays and Cybele,* for example, is full of references to the Roman myth of Cybele and Attis. An audience that is unable to fit these references into the development of the story will find the total effect of the movie to be ambiguous and ultimately unsatisfactory.

It would be an overstatement to say that a particular audience must be able to grasp all denotations and connotations of the subject matter. Still it is true to say understanding, even on a most literal level, is directly proportionate to the meaningfulness of film content. A touchstone you might use to gauge the understanding of the literal sense of the movie is found in the ability of the viewers to synopsize the film. If they cannot do this or do it in a confused way, chances are they have not grasped even the surface idea of the picture.

(c) *Author:* A third point of view is that of the film maker himself toward the subject matter. The world of reality is not something restricted to creative artists; all of us are aware that life has its joys and sufferings, that men are motivated for this or that reason, that our actions meet with success and failure, and on and on. A creative artist differs from most of us in his desire to make some statement about these things. He has an insight, some personal understanding he thinks is of value that he wants to communicate to us. We gain our understanding of his ideas by observing the way he approaches his chosen subject matter. What does he select or reject from the world around him? Having limited his potential subject

matter, what emphasis or de-emphasis does he give to
the remaining material? Finally, how does he manipulate his film content according to the technical factors
of movie making? That is to say, does he give special
meaning to content by use of light and shadow, camera
angles, and editing? Anyone acquainted with *Citizen
Kane* will recognize immediately how important film
technique can be in presenting the director's particular attitude toward his subject matter.

Deeper understanding of a particular movie can
sometimes be gained by considering factors outside
of the picture itself. By comparing a particular film
under discussion with other works of the film maker,
you may discover him treating similar material. The
better you become acquainted with his style and come
to know his general outlook on life, the deeper will
be your understanding of each successive film. Sometimes, as in the case of the Apu trilogy of Satyajit
Ray, a succession of films is necessary to grasp the
total idea of the film maker. Fellini makes so many
references to *La Dolce Vita* in *8½* that one would be
at a distinct disadvantage had he not seen one before
the other.

Further hints into the thinking of a film maker can
be had by considering outside influences that have a
bearing upon him. What, for example, are other creative artists saying about the same subject matter?
What is his attitude toward their work, and their attitude toward his? What are the general social, political and economic pressures brought upon him from
his studio and from the society in which he lives?

These and other questions are valuable for arriving
at a more definitive critical statement concerning a
film maker and his work. For the purposes of most
film society discussions, however, the essential area
of discussion should remain with the particular picture at hand. When you have exhausted all the poten-

tial information to be found in the dramatic structure of the content and the various film making techniques employed within the picture, then, if time remains, it is valuable to discuss outside influences.

(d) *Society:* Occasionally it happens that a picture is of such import in the urgency and treatment of its subject matter that it has an influence upon the community as a whole. Films of political and social realism were used during the thirties to affect deliberate attitudes. The Soviet and Nazi film industry had a total impact far beyond the actual viewers of their pictures. When you are discussing a propaganda film, then, it is important to remember that it was made to have meaning that extends to the whole community.

American pictures, though sometimes obviously didactic in treatment, generally cannot be thought of as propaganda films in the sense described above. Still there pervades a general outlook on manners and morals that serves in the last analysis to sway minds as effectively as do propaganda films. It would be difficult, however, to point the finger at any particular American film and say that it was this film that led to this or that general attitude of mind. Rather it must be noted that American films tend more to reflect already-existing social patterns than to institute them. Horatio Alger-and-Cinderella thinking was not begun by Hollywood, but the American movie has done its fair share in keeping it alive.

Thus far the treatment of "film meaning" has been considered in a general way. Awareness of this question of "meaning: for whom?" is valuable for you in conducting an organized approach to discussion. It is not necessary, of course, that you limit the discussion to only one point of view; but it is important that someone taking part in the discussion realizes when the group is moving from one viewpoint to another.

Within your discussion of the various points of view there are several specific elements that should be brought out. The following seven points, though probably not exhaustive, should serve as suitable starting points for a specific approach to "movie understanding".

1. Subject Matter

This is the elemental raw stuff upon which a film is built. It can vary from real persons and events to imaginary places and things. The objects of a movie can come from the exterior world: things, nature, animals and men viewed from the outside—a descriptive representation of reality; or it can come from an interior world: a world of human sentiments, ideas and passions — a psychological representation of reality.

When treating of subject matter it is important to remember that it often has a relevance to a particular time and place. The mutiny and mutineers Eisenstein dealt with in *Potemkin* had a real intellectual and emotional relevance to the Russian audience of 1925, while mutiny and mutineers of the *Bounty* have not meant much to an American audience either in 1935 or 1963. A didactic picture, moreover, treating of specific social or economic evil tends to lose its urgency with the passage of time. Many American movies of the depression era now appear a bit naive in their economic notions. At the time of their initial release, however, they were intellectual and emotional challenges to the audience.

Subject matter, then, can be anything, anywhere, at any time. For your discussions, the important question to consider is why did the film maker choose this particular subject matter in order to communicate his ideas?

2. Synopsis

Bare subject matter is not enough, characters must say and do something, events must happen and have consequences. By means of a synopsis you are able to have a survey of action and dramatic structure. A film maker displays his particular attitude toward his subject matter by the way he manipulates the action. So, for example, a poor man in the midst of some economic crisis can be led through a series of events so manipulated by a film maker that his freedom to choose is denied him and he is led ultimately to despair. While another might lead a similar man through adversities that ultimately strengthen his character and bring him to an understanding of his personal worth. Poverty motivates action in both *Gervaise* and *Bicycle Thief*, yet character development and dramatic resolution are much different.

3. Theme

It is with the theme that a movie takes on its particular character and gains its significance. *High Noon*, for example, uses subject matter, characters and plot development of the standard western; yet the theme that writer Carl Foreman and director Fred Zinnemann choose to treat makes the movie quite different from the traditional Friday night "shoot-em-up". A surface story can be simple; still thematic motivation, ideas implied rather than expressed, can give it depth and dimension.

4. Characters

Persons to whom events happen are obviously necessary to any story development. They serve as important keys to understanding the ideas of a film maker. Sympathetic characterization will lead the viewer to an affinity with the ideas and conclusions of the picture. Thus, authority portrayed as rational and virile will lead to a positive attitude toward law and order; while authority wielded by buffoons or tyrants produces sympathy with those who take the law into their own hands.

Sometimes it happens that the personality of the actor himself is so strong that we are not able to get beyond him to the character of the story. In the *Cain Mutiny*, for example, one leaves the theater remarking that Captain Queeg is more Bogart than a character from Wouk's novel. Directors will use a strong movie personality or stereotyped characterizations in order to impress some specific point. The movie-actress caricature in *La Dolce Vita* is a good example of well controlled use of stereotype. Poor use of stereotypes generally indicates that the film maker really has nothing to say and is merely padding his picture with character and situational bromides.

Since characterization is so open to manipulation, a very valid point for your discussion is "Why does the director develop the characters in this manner?"

5. Genre and Style

Meaning of content and theme is further influenced by the generic category a film maker chooses to use. The same subject matter can be approached seriously or comically; it can be presented on an epic scale or limited to simple melodrama. Style also affects like subject matter in diverse ways; hence, the personal outlook of a film maker will direct his approach to realism or romanticism. Generally speaking, the film maker's attitude toward life will lead him to specialize in one of the major generic categories. Since it would be beyond the scope of this book to do more than suggest possible areas for study and discussion, the following outline treatment of film genres is designed to give you possible starting points for your future work. Please keep in mind that these divisions are found by analyzing many motion pictures. In your analysis of a particular movie you may find a certain overlapping of genres; however, one genre will tend to dominate the approach of the film maker.

For purposes of analysis, then, movies can be said to belong to one of five major categories:

(a) *Realist:* A film maker tends to approach his subject matter in an objective and impartial manner. Although he remains an artist, who selects and rejects from the world of reality, still he aims to have his work maintain a fidelity to reality. He is driven by the desire to communicate to others the actuality of the persons and events that surround us.

(b) *Tragic:* A director who is particularly sensitive to life and death, to joys and sufferings and to love and hatred will color his subject matter in such a way as to bring out the serious aspects of reality. He magnifies, distorts, diminishes and in multiple other ways subjects the world of reality to his particular point of view. His attention may focus on the "tragedy of events" with an emphasis on environmental influences or he may limit his attention to "personal tragedy" by considering the consequences attendant upon human decisions. Whether his film will be drama in the classic sense or will be mere melodrama depends upon the worth of his raw subject matter and his own personal talents.

(c) *Comic:* A director who uses a comic approach to his subject matter is not ignorant of the serious elements of life, but he prefers to make his comment on life by appealing to those things in human existence that are humorous. Farce, satire, romance and musical comedy become the avenues through which a director presents his ideas.

(d) *Epic:* A director approaches his subject matter in terms of heroic actions where human endeavors and forces of nature are presented on a grand scale.

Often the subject matter is drawn from legend and folklore and so treated that the epic confrontation appeals to the sociological and sentimental instincts of modern man. An epic confrontation can take place between man and nature, man and society or between peoples in war and revolution.

To a significant degree, the American western can be thought of as belonging to the epic genre. Cowboys and the great West possess epic qualities that can be accentuated or limited according to a director's point of view. While the western is a unique contribution of Hollywood to movie making, its spirit and vitality lead to imitations by other countries. At present, for example, some of the best westerns are being produced in Japan.

(e) *Poetic:* Sometimes a director will break away from the essential realism of motion pictures in order to concentrate upon poetic values. This does not mean that he merely glamorizes an essentially realistic situation; rather, he accentuates the lyric elements of his subject matter. This poetic point of view can operate within a realistic context as in *Black Orpheus, Wild Strawberries,* and *Last Year at Marienbad;* or it can turn to a context of the marvelous as Jean Cocteau does in his *Beauty and the Beast.*

Awareness of genre, then, will help you in your analysis of a particular picture, since it serves to give you hints into a film maker's attitude toward his present subject matter and, further, it hints at his general outlook on reality.

6. Social Values

As a product of a given country, produced at a given time, movies stand as a commentary on the society that produces and consumes them. Of all the arts, motion pictures are most sensitive to the social values of a particular time and place. Film historians tell us that the career of D. W. Griffith came to an end, not because he had lost his talent, but because his pictures no longer reflected the attitudes of the audience. The symbiotic relationship between motion pictures and society makes it imperative that you keep in mind the country of origin and time of production in your search for understanding what a film maker is trying to say. Manifestly, the values of an American audience in 1964 are not valid yardsticks with which to measure a Russian film of the 1920's.

7. *Total Personality of a Film*

Each movie has the right to be judged as a total artistic experience. The foregoing factors are valuable for purposes of analysis and discussion, but one does not approach a movie with these elements in the forefront of his mind. As with a symphony that is not completed until the final note is played, so too, a movie is not completed until the final picture has faded from the screen. It is hoped that your ability to carefully analyze a movie will develop your cinema sensibilities so that significant motion pictures will become a rewarding human experience for you.

IV

A Sample Series
of Films

Background

The purpose of this section is to provide for the reader a model film series that has unity of purpose and lends itself to discussion and learning. The series offered in this chapter will illustrate one way in which a specialized program can be organized and presented in a meaningful way. Many film groups may feel that the theme approach does not suit the needs of their membership and will prefer other series or even a different approach (consult Appendix C for other suggestions).[5]

The program notes presented on each film of the following series are generally more complete than most study groups would want, but enough material is provided so that each group might choose what it feels would be best adapted for its own audience in case the series should be selected for a program.

It has not been the intention of this book to provide film societies with program notes on any large number of films. Program notes are undoubtedly of great value, even essential to the success of a serious film group, but to supply notes on more than these six films is beyond the scope of this book. Furthermore, program notes are available from several

[5] The type of films in this series may be too difficult for high school groups; for high school programs, *High Noon*, *On the Waterfront* and *La Strada* might be retained. Others that might be substituted: *Ox-Bow Incident*, *The Burmese Harp* and *East of Eden*.

sources cited in an appendix.[6] The best solution to
the immediate need for program notes is for each
group to make its own, as Chapter III has suggested.

"The Individual Choice and Its Consequences" is
a series of films whose focus is on the essentially dramatic action of personal choice and its consequences
for the individual and his society. Traditionally the
crux of choice has been at the core of Western drama;
even an existentialist hero can sum up his own tragedy
with the statement: "You are your life, and nothing
else." For man's life will be summarized at the point
of death by the values that he has chosen to follow.
Although a man may be guided and even limited in
this choice by his environment, his own capacities, or
the power of a destiny or Providence outside himself,
nevertheless, the choice is still essentially his own.

The films that make up the series all revolve about
a choice of the individual, whether that choice is made
in the spotlight of public life or in the hidden re-
cesses of his heart. The choice will be treated in a
quite different manner in each film because the film
originated from individual artists and will be carried
out according to the vision of each film maker. The
study of each film of the series must concentrate, then,
not alone on the theme of choice but on how this theme
has been translated into the film medium. It is in this
kind of careful study that an audience can grow in its
appreciation and critical judgment of motion pictures.

A final point about the series. Some film societies
may find that a specialized program like this one does
not appeal to a sufficiently wide audience to secure
proper financial support. In this case the six films
of the special series might be incorporated into a
larger program of a dozen or fifteen films, for which
season tickets can be sold. Some of the more inter-

---

[6] Consult Appendix A for addresses of these sources.

ested people from the larger audience can attend the discussions on the six films of the series that form a unified theme. This can be done with many series in which financial problems dictate the selection of a wider variety of films.[7]

There can be two extremes in film criticism and consequently in discussions of films: there are the humanists who are interested only in theme and content and who ignore any question of technique; then there are the film buffs who are so concerned with form that content is almost totally ignored. Such divergent tendencies need not force the discussion into absolute categories nor complete disjunctions. A film study group should be concerned with *both* form and content and though the distinction between the two is necessary for the sake of clarity, it should not create a breakdown of communications nor ruin a discussion. The following notes are meant to combine both views and espouse no particular school of criticism. It is hoped that they may provide helpful guidelines for deepening appreciation and sharpening judgment.

The order for showing the series should be followed when possible:

I *High Noon* directed by Fred Zinnemann (1952)

II *La Strada* directed by Federico Fellini (1954)

III *On the Waterfront* directed by Elia Kazan (1954)

IV *Ikiru* directed by Akira Kurosawa (1952)

V *The Set-Up* directed by Robert Wise (1949)

VI *The Diary of a Country Priest* directed by Robert Bresson (1951)

----

[7] Consult Appendix B under programming to see what the University of Illinois Film Society did in a case like this.

I. High Noon

American, 1952. Directed by Fred Zinnemann. Produced by Stanley Kramer. Screenplay by Carl Foreman from a story "The Tin Star" by John W. Cunningham. Music by Dimitri Tiomkin. Photographed by Floyd Crosby. Starring Gary Cooper, Thomas Mitchell, Grace Kelly, Katy Jurado, Lloyd Bridges, Otto Kruger, Lon Chaney, Henry Morgan.

Background: the Western

It is a fact of film history—which the Hollywood industry has not ignored—that since its beginning the western has been a perennial favorite with audiences. In their attempt to explain this box-office phenomenon, critics have suggested that the basic idealism of the genre appealed to the American need for a hero; or that the hero was a modern Everyman; or that (in the Freudian phase of criticism) the gun-toting cowboy who generally shied away from women was a symbolic expression of some deep psychic fixation in our national character; or, finally, that the western was simply the most exciting type of film entertainment ever invented and therefore was bound to hold the interest of people looking for excitement and action.

The western seems to be particularly well adapted to the film medium with its emphasis on physical action, suspense, chases, fights and the natural setting in the wide open spaces. All of these factors help to form a strong stereotype for the western. As one practitioner of the western movie script summed up after years of work in the trade, there are three things any good western must have: a fist fight, a chase on horseback and a gun battle.

Over the years since Edwin S. Porter's *The Great Train Robbery*, the western has developed through many stages and has seen heroes come and go. It was

after World War II, however, that the genre was first
able to depart from stereotype and create some of the
western's most outstanding achievements. This new
kind of western that developed after 1945 was due in
part to the war, which shattered so many illusions
and gave an impetus toward greater realism in character and plot. Up to this time the western had tended
to idealize and stereotype its characters. This ideali-
zation had been given a great thrust by the introduction of the epic western with James Cruze's *The
Covered Wagon* (1923) and John Ford's *The Iron
Horse* (1924) and *Stagecoach* (1939). It was not until 1945 that the western became something more than
an epic or a simple adventure story. Ford's *My Darling
Clementine* (1947) indicated that the director was
aware of a change of attitude in the audience and
was capable of adapting to this new realism. Henry
King's *The Gunfighter* (1950), Fred Zinnemann's
High Noon (1952) and George Stevens' *Shane* (1953)
showed that the genre had changed radically since the
days of William S. Hart and Johnny Mack Brown.

The success of *High Noon* was instant and has continued through the first decade of its history. There
were several peculiarities that set the film apart from
other westerns, even among its contemporaries. Critics immediately nominated it as a classic of its genre
and yet admitted that it was not really a western. Another curious fact of its history is that women generally liked it, a rarity among the regular cowboy
movies. The authors of a recent history of the western
sum up the film: "The most acclaimed and most in-
fluential western of the past decade, *High Noon* offered a strong dramatic role to Gary Cooper and an
appealing title song. The film was a smash success at
the box office. It has been, however, somewhat overrated, since its script was inauthentic, too modern,
displaying little knowledge of the real conditions of

the old West. Its direction was over-studied, but a major cinematic asset was the creative editing of Elmo Williams." [8] Whatever the reasons for its success, there can be no doubt that *High Noon* has taken its place in the long history of the westerns.

The Picture

Time is such an important factor in the structure of *High Noon* that it almost seems to usurp more than its share of the audience's attention. Zinnemann's constant use of clocks and references to time as a means of building suspense may appear to be over-done, but it is evidently more than a gimmick in the mind of the director. The actual story time in the film is 85 minutes, from 10:40 a.m. until approximately 12:05 noon; and this coincides exactly with the time the film takes to run, 85 minutes. This unity of story time and running time gives the film a concentration and austerity that it could not otherwise have had. There is simply no time to attend to scenery or sub-plots. Frank Miller will arrive at noon, and there will be immediate retribution, one way or the other. Time, indeed, seems to force unity of place as well as of action.

Given this highly concentrated structure, what has Zinnemann done to translate the story into meaning-ful images? He has incorporated time into the image of the clock, but not that alone. He reminds the audi-ence of the clock in repeated shots of it on the walls of offices, of the hotel lobby and in homes. The mar-shal asks people what time it is or reminds others of the hour. The shadows of buildings and of people in the streets become sundials to remind the viewer in a more subtle way of the inexorable passage of time.

---

[8] George Fenin and W. K. Everson, *The Western: From Silents to Cinerama* (New York: Orion Press, 1962), p. 335.

Photographically the director is too shrewd simply to repeat shots to indicate a passage of time without introducing some significant variations. For example, as the camera returns again and again to the three killers waiting at the station for their leader to arrive, the audience gets a slightly different view of the railroad tracks each time. At first the audience looks down the tracks with the waiting men from the far right, approximately from where the men are lounging. But each time this shot is repeated, the camera has taken up a new position farther to the left, so that just before the train is heard approaching in the distance, it is looking directly down the empty tracks from a low angle. The audience sees the parallel rails seemingly meet at the point of infinity out on the prairie. In this image Zinnemann has captured both the loneliness of the marshal and the inevitability of what noon will bring.

The basic dramatic conflict of the film is not, as in most westerns, between the marshal and the badmen. Rather it is between the marshal's decision to do his duty and the community which fails to back him in his action. *High Noon* is the story of an individual who finds himself standing absolutely alone against the crowd. As a point of historical fact, Carl Foreman wrote the script for the screenplay soon after he was arraigned before the famous Committee on Un-American Affairs that came to Hollywood in the early fifties. Foreman has said of the script: "I used a western background to tell a story of a community corrupted by fear, with implications that I hoped would be obvious to almost everyone who saw the film, at least in America."

An audience must be alerted that *High Noon* is not simply a study of the western lawman, the superhuman hero who overcomes all obstacles to conquer a threatening evil. The real evil of the picture is not, as has been pointed out, the badmen but rather the effect of fear and compromise in a community. It is the marshal's story, to be sure, but all that he has to do is to carry out his duty in the tradition of the western lawman. The story ends traditionally with a piece of bravura that is far less convincing in its realism than the previous eighty minutes of suspense, cowardice, betrayal and final loneliness of the marshal.

The marshal in the story is not the usual lone wolf of the western. He is married in the first ten minutes of the film and seems to have the good will of the whole town; yet as the story advances, the marshal experiences a growing isolation. It is not an extraordinary situation, of course, to have the sheriff face the badmen singlehanded; for the hero is that much more heroic. But in *High Noon* the isolation rather cuts the other way and makes those who are absent seem that much more cowardly. The late critic Robert Warshow has pointed out this peculiarity of the film: "The technical problem was to make it necessary for the marshal to face his enemies alone; to explain *why* the other townspeople are not at his side is to raise a question which does not exist in the proper frame of the western movie, where the hero is 'naturally' alone and it is only necessary to contrive the physical absence of those who might be his allies, if any contrivance is needed at all." [9]

High Noon tells why the marshal is alone and in so doing shows that far from being a classic of the western form, it is a story of a fear-ridden community, in short, a kind of social drama in western clothes.

To say that *High Noon* is not a "classic" western, however, is not to say that the film does not have merit. Zinnemann achieves a number of notable successes with his integration of direction, acting, music

---

[9] Robert Warshow, *The Immediate Experience* (New York: Doubleday, 1962), p. 149.

and editing into a powerful whole. His suspense is achieved with a good use of clocks and time metaphors. He makes his commentary with expressive camera positions (for instance, as the camera looks down on the marshal standing in the noonday sun in the empty street one gets the sense of the isolation of the man). The editorial cutting has only been mentioned, but it plays a great part in the impact of the film, especially in the last twenty minutes. The music has perhaps been overrated but it is important to the creation of mood in the picture. All of these elements have been assembled with a care and exactness by the director, and the result is a good if not classic western.

One might pose a final question: Does the mixture of the western with the film of social consciousness make the best kind of combination? One feels that the exciting final gunfight is too pat a way to cover up the fact that though the badmen are dead at the film's close, the real evil within the community has not really been purged but only put aside for a time.

How to Present High Noon

In a discussion of *High Noon* one should certainly first try to understand the basic story-line and the skill with which Zinnemann has translated this into cinematic terms. The discussion leader should not try to run through every item of film language that the film employs, but there are areas that are worth noting: the use of time-suspense images and techniques; the far greater emphasis on editing to give the film a sense of tension and movement; and the use of music and sound to tell the story.

The group might, after considering the technical qualities, concentrate its attention on the basic structure and meaning of the film. If the film is the first one shown in the series and people are unacquainted with any kind of organized discussion of films, the leader should try to draw out the basic conflict in the story by asking a question: Who is the hero in the film and who the antagonist? If *High Noon* is simply another western, the answer is obvious; but if it is something more, the easy pairing off of hero and villain is not quite as easy. Hadleyville itself is perhaps more the villain than the killer, Frank Miller. Then the leader might focus on the problem of the individual against the crowd, the conformity of the mass of people to domination by fear.

In case the group leader finds that his first discussion is wandering because the method is unfamiliar to the participants, he might pose some more specific questions: In how many different ways did the director convey the sense of passing time? How often were clocks used? Did this seem overdone? Was the musical score integral to the film? Was the ballad helpful or not? Why? A great deal has been said by critics about the editing (consult Chapter II for a brief discussion of this term). Find and discuss examples of good editing technique in the film. What were some of the elements that made the film a genuine western? What were some of the elements that made it different from most westerns? What is the marshal's crucial choice and why is it so opposed to the community who all seem to be fairly good people? How is this conflict at odds with that of the average western? Does it reflect a problem in contemporary society?

II. La Strada

Italian, 1954. Directed by Federico Fellini. Produced by Dino de Laurentiis and Carlo Ponti. Screenplay and original story by Fellini and Tullio Pinelli. Music by Nino Rota. Photographed by Otello Martelli. Starring Giulietta Masina, Anthony Quinn, Richard Basehart, Aldo Silvani.

Background: the Films of Federico Fellini

Federico Fellini grew up with the Italian neo-realism of the 1940's as a scriptwriter. He collaborated with the first line of neo-realist directors: Germi in *Mafia* (1948), *El Commino della Separanza* (1950), *Il Brigante di Taccadi Lupo* (1951); Lattuda in *Without Pity* (1947) and *Il Mulino de Pó* (1948); Alessandrini in *Chi l'ha Visto* (1943) and *L'Erbeo errante* (1947). But it was with the most outstanding director of that time that Fellini was most closely associated, Roberto Rossellini. He helped to script Rossellini's *Open City* (1945), *Paisan* (1946), *Flowers of St. Francis* (1950) and *Europa 51* (1951).

There can be no doubt that Fellini has been influenced by the directors with whom he worked, but when he became a director himself, he was accused of betraying the cause of neo-realism. Fellini denied this charge and maintained that he still was in the main stream of neo-realism, as he understood the movement. His own definition of this postwar Italian movement helps to clarify the thinking behind Fellini's own brand of neo-realism. He says: "For me, neo-realism is not a question of *what* you show—its spirit is in *how* you show it. It's just a way of looking around, without convention or prejudice. Certain people still think neo-realism is fit to show only certain kinds of reality; and they insist that this is social reality. But in this way, it becomes mere propaganda . . . People have written that I am a traitor to the cause of neo-realism, that I am too much of an individualist, too much of an individual."[10]

Fellini is a highly autobiographical film maker

---

[10] Gideon Bachmann's interview with Fellini appearing in Robert Hughes' (ed.) *Film: Book I: The Audience and the Filmmaker* (New York: Grove Press, 1959), p. 100.

whose work reflects his personal philosophy and experiences. He says in the same interview mentioned above: "I cannot remove myself from the content of my films . . . What usually starts me on a film idea is that something happens to me which I think has some bearing on other people's experiences. And the feeling is usually the same: to try first of all to tell something about myself; and in so doing, to try to find a salvation, to try to find a road toward some meaning, some truth, something that will be important to others, too." [11] The personal note in Fellini's films is evident in his work from *Footlights* (1950) to *8½* (1963).

Fellini began directing in 1950 with *Footlights* (*Luci del Varietá*), in which he starred his wife, Giulietta Masina, who was destined to become something of a Fellini trademark in the next few years. His next film, *The White Shiek* (1952), demonstrated some of Fellini's potentialities as a humorist, especially in caricaturing the popular fads of contemporary society. He contributed a brief sketch, "The Matrimonial Agency", to an anthology film called *Love in the City* (1953) and finished in the same year his first serious film, *I Vitelloni*, about a group of young drifters in a provincial Italian city. *La Strada* (1954) has been praised by many critics as Fellini's masterpiece. His next film after this was *The Swindle* (*Il Bidone*, 1955), which suffered by comparison with its predecessor, though it merits much more attention than it got. *In Nights of Cabiria* (1957) Fellini began to move into a city society, more sophisticated but no less human than his previous stories of entertainers and drifters.

The director took three years to complete his next undertaking, a massive film chronicle of modern so-

---

[11] *Ibid.*, p. 102.

ciety, *La Dolce Vita* (1960). It received a sensational reception in Europe and the United States. Whatever Fellini had been trying to say about society seems to have found expression in this epic study of people adrift in the modern world of prosperity and despair. As a reaction to a great deal of misunderstanding and criticism of *La Dolce Vita*, Fellini created an episode for the anthology film, *Boccaccio 70* (1961). His attack on the puritanical mind in "The Dream of Dr. Antonio" begins with a basically humorous situation but loses its effect by unduly extending the episode. The director carried his autobiographical tendency to its logical conclusions in *8½* and made a film about himself making a film. Granted that the effort is a real *tour de force* of technique, one questions whether it will stand up to some of the earlier films, where Fellini's poetry of human feelings is much less burdened with technique than in this film. One may well ask: Where does Fellini go from here?

The Picture

Fellini himself has given a hint of the underlying problem in *La Strada*. In the interview already quoted, he answered the question about the philosophy behind his films by saying: "Well, I could tell you what for me is one of the most pressing problems, one which provides part of the theme for all my films. It's the terrible difficulty people have in talking to each other —the old problem of communication, the desperate anguish to be *with*, the desire to have a real, authentic relationship with another person . . . It may be that I'll change, but for now [1959] I'm completely absorbed in this problem—maybe because I have not yet solved it in my private life."[12]

---

[12] *Ibid.*, p. 101.

The problem of interpersonal relationships is not the whole of *La Strada*, of course, but it may provide a starting point for seeing the basic struggle in this allegory of "the road". Gelsomina's one aim is to love, to be *with* Zampano; but love demands interchange and Zampano seems quite incapable of this, trapped as he is within the narrow world of his animal nature. The Fool compares him to a dog who cannot communicate except by barking. At a crucial point in the film, the Fool convinces Gelsomina that her destiny is to break through the barrier and teach Zampano to be a human being. The cry of Zampano as he claws the sand at the end of the film is not that of a wounded beast but the anguish of a human person in his birth pangs.

In terms of visual images, Fellini has succeeded in fusing poetic symbol and grim reality, just as he has created characters who are at once concrete individuals and symbolic figures. A Christian interpretation of the symbolism in *La Strada* is reinforced by the Christian context of Fellini's milieu and background. It has been suggested that the Fool is a Christ symbol. This suggestion is built upon several interesting coincidences: the Fool first appears in angel's wings high above Gelsomina and the mass of people in the piazza; he convinces Gelsomina that all things have a purpose in the mind of God; he predicts his own death; Zampano drags his body over the grass in a cruciform fashion; he is finally buried in a cave-like culvert. Gelsomina, perhaps, embodies the element of conscience as it works to humanize the brutal destructive forces represented by Zampano.

There is a danger in interpreting a film in this way. For a person can hunt out images that will help to make the film say what he wants it to say. Keeping this danger in mind, one can, nevertheless, find Fellini using images that seem to bear an interpretation in the spiritual order. At the very least, each viewer should try to discover some unity in the images that the film maker has set before him.

Despite the lyrical mood of *La Strada*, Fellini has remained in the neo-realistic setting of the street. The photography is done on location, and these locations are carefully chosen to reinforce the mood of each scene. The empty piazza, the seashore, the grimy cheapness of a *cafe economica* are part of Fellini's inheritance from postwar directors like Rossellini. But the scenes are much more than a record of the social strata in which the characters live. Fellini seems able to evoke from the very locations themselves a poetry that is as eloquent as that of his actors. One may recall the feeling of desolation and loneliness that the empty, litter-strewn piazza conveys when Fellini pictures it late at night after the carnival crowd has left. It is in the fusion of setting and characters that Fellini is able to create a unified whole that is expressive of his particular vision of life.

How to Present La Strada

There are several practical suggestions to be made about the showing of *La Strada*. First, since this has been a very popular film, some prints are quite worn; therefore, it would be advisable to carefully preview the film for any mechanical difficulties such as breaks or poor sound. Second, since the film is lyrical and depends to some extent upon the continuation of the mood once it has been created, the use of two projectors to avoid a reel break is desirable.

The discussion leader should have the group make a careful examination of Fellini's visual imagery. For example, is it not true to say that Fellini's locations perform three functions in the film: to present a realistic setting in lower class Italian life, to set the particular mood of the scene or at least reinforce it, and to symbolize something beyond the immediate confines of the story? Discuss specifically the use of music in two ways: to set the mood in certain key scenes and even to give a certain structural unity to the film as a whole, much in the manner of a lyric poem.

Regarding theme, what does Fellini think about woman's relationship to man? Is she an instrument of his salvation or destruction, his fulfillment or frustration? In discussing this, the members of the group may be able to throw light on elements of *La Strada* by bringing in a knowledge of some of Fellini's other films—though the discussion should not get away from *La Strada*'s story and theme. If one agrees that Gelsomina's decision to remain with Zampano is the turning point in the film, is her death to be considered a tragic waste or a redemptive sacrifice? How explain either interpretation?

III. On the Waterfront

American, 1954. Directed by Elia Kazan. Produced by Sam Spiegel. Story by Budd Schulberg. Music by Leonard Bernstein. Photographed by Boris Kaufman. Starring Marlon Brando, Eva Marie Saint, Karl Malden, Lee J. Cobb, Rod Steiger, Pat Henning.

Background: Kazan and the Film of Social Consciousness

One might say that the American film first became aware of its social responsibilities when the Great Depression forced Americans to face up to their problems. It was Warner Brothers who, in 1930, led the way toward greater realism with its policy of basing as many of its movies as possible on spot news and headline stories. It was Warner's *Little Caesar* (1930), *The Public Enemy* (1931) and *I Am a Fugitive from a Chain Gang* (1932) that initiated several cycles of Hollywood films and was ultimately responsible for establishing two genres that have had a strong influence on American and world film making. The first was the gangster film or, more broadly speaking, the *film noir,* as the French have aptly named it. The second was the film of social consciousness.

Mervyn LeRoy's *I Am a Fugitive from a Chain Gang* was the prototype of the film whose social protest had repercussions beyond the immediate confines of the moviehouse. This film introduced American audiences to serious social problems that had no facile answer. The positive response to films like LeRoy's was a heartening sign that audiences were not coming to the theaters just to escape the grim reality of 1932. Standing at the end of the important decade of the 1930's, Lewis Jacobs wrote in 1939 that: "The graveness of the past ten years has seen the content of movies take on a more serious tone. A depression-hit America has focused the movies' attention upon social corruption, economic discrepancies, political maladjustments, and has started a search for a code of personal and social values that will not rest entirely on sex and affluence. . . . The movies are showing a tendency to participate more openly in world issues with a new fearlessness and with a maturity of thought that augers a great future." [13]

It is difficult to say whether Jacobs' expectations would have been fulfilled or not, for the Second World War intervened. Thus was broken a tradition of social-minded films that began in 1932 with *Chain Gang* and continued through the 1930's with others like

---

[13] Lewis Jacobs, *The Rise of the American Film* (New York: Harcourt, Brace and Co., 1939), p. 538.

Black Legion (1936), *They Won't Forget* (1937) and *Grapes of Wrath* (1940). After the war a cycle of films on the problem of prejudice emerged from a restless American public who were anxious to face their own social problems. It included Dmytryk's *Crossfire* (1947), Kazan's *Gentleman's Agreement* (1947) and *Pinky* (1949), Kramer and DeRouchement's *Home of the Brave* (1949) and *Lost Boundaries* (1950), Brown's *Intruder in the Dust* (1949) and Losey's *The Lawless* (1950). There were certainly other films of social awareness during this period, but the prejudice films formed one of the most outstanding examples of a cycle of films on an important social theme.

With the advent of television, the Hollywood film industry underwent a number of changes that affected the production of the cycle films. The gangster and social-protest films (and one could include the western too) seem to have had their best development in the second-feature departments of the large studios. It was in this environment that a great number of films were made on small budgets, which allowed for greater creativity than was possible in the production of expensive blockbusters. After 1950 when the major studios began to lose their position of dominance and second features disappeared, the genre film took on a new look. The gangster film virtually yielded the field to its television counterpart. The film of social consciousness certainly continued, but it was usually a "big" film with star actors and well-known directors and producers, working independently of the studios. Stanley Kramer was responsible for the production of a number of such films: *Champion* (1949), *The Men* (1950), *Death of a Salesman* (1951), *The Wild One* (1954), *The Defiant Ones* (1958) and *On the Beach* (1959).

One director who has been concerned with social

problems since the beginning of his career in Hollywood is Elia Kazan. Many of the sixteen films that he has made over the past twenty years betray the director's concern with society's problems. One may get a feeling of Kazan's concerns by recalling his film work: *A Tree Grows in Brooklyn* (1945), *Boomerang* (1947), *The Sea of Grass* (1947), *Gentleman's Agreement* (1947), *Pinky* (1949), *Panic in the Streets* (1950), *A Streetcar Named Desire* (1951), *Viva Zapata* (1952), *Man on a Tightrope* (1953), *On the Waterfront* (1954), *East of Eden* (1955), *Baby Doll* (1956), *A Face in the Crowd* (1957), *Wild River* (1960), *Splendor in the Grass* (1961), *America, America* (1963).

If Kazan's films often tackle genuine problems in American society, they are not off-beat, low-budget productions but expensive films with well-known stars. This is not to say that it is impossible to make a sincere film of social consciousness under these circumstances. Still, there are difficulties. Films like *On the Waterfront, East of Eden* and *Wild River* are certainly in a different class from low-budget films with a social dimension like Kirshner's *The Hoodlum Priest* (1961) or MacKenzie's *The Exiles* (1962). Money, of course, is not the only difference but it is an important one. One suspects that when a director or producer is spending a million dollars of someone else's money, considerations of the box office are going to weigh more heavily in the scale than in a more modest production.

The genre of protest films has evolved a great deal over the decades since *Chain Gang*, but the film of social consciousness still continues to issue from Hollywood and from a growing number of independent producers and directors. Perhaps the most significant films still come from "below", i.e., from non-Hollywood American sources; one thinks of Sidney Meyer's

The Quiet One (1948), Kent MacKenzie's *The Exiles* (1962) and Lionel Rogosin's *On the Bowery* (1955).

The Picture

On the Waterfront's greatest asset is the realistic milieu that it creates for its characters by its documentary approach. Filmed on location in Brooklyn and the Hoboken dock area, the picture was able to capture the surface reality of the locations with a great deal of fidelity and imagination. Boris Kaufman, a cameraman of long experience, has exposed the monotonous rows of brick apartments with their cluttered roofs, the dingy neighborhood beer halls and the drab physiognomy of Brooklyn in winter. Yet out of this he has created a beauty by the composition of his pictures and the sensitive combination of light and shadow. Scene after scene rings true pictorially for an audience nurtured on the neo-realist fidelity to *mise-en-scène* of many European postwar films. One thinks of many images in *Waterfront*: the bare little park in front of the grim turn-of-the-century Catholic church, the narrowness of the Doyle's apartment, the gray overcast of New York harbor in November, the jumble of lines, chimneys and ledges on the rooftops of the apartments. These visual images give the film an important strength that no other weakness can entirely dissipate.

Kazan's experience on the stage, especially with the method of Actors' Studio, has helped to evoke strong performances from his actors: Marlon Brando (academy award for the part), Rod Steiger, Eva Marie Saint (academy award) and Karl Malden. Lee J. Cobb begins well but toward the end one wonders if all the shouting is really necessary to show how upset he is. The Method acting of many of the cast would seem well-suited to the realism of the surroundings. Terry's halting, unfinished sentences, hunching and shuffling seem appropriate to his character and blend well with the milieu. Eddy with her parochial-school-girl outlook stands in contrast with Terry, yet seems quite real in the situation. Karl Malden's face is as blunt and eloquently unbeautiful as his acting in his portrayal of Father Barry.

The pictorial naturalness and the realism of much of the acting seem to fit uneasily with the score by Leonard Bernstein. The musical accompaniment at times is too dramatic, almost operatic, for the low-keyed realism of the visual images. Drums and a crescendo from a symphony orchestra may be appropriate to *Gone With the Wind* or *Lawrence of Arabia,* but they stand out conspicuously on the Hoboken docks. Fortunately, this is not a constant threat to the film's unity.

Kazan's flare for the dramatic scene sometimes misfires and gives the film occasional scenes that are out of keeping with the realism of the story's material. The most glaring example of this is the ending of the film which is frankly melodramatic. Though there is nothing wrong with melodrama in itself, it does not mix well with the documentary approach that the film otherwise espouses.

Much of Kazan's dramatic instinct, however, is useful in the film because it is concentrated on the personal story of Terry Maloy and not simply on the documentary aspects of waterfront racketeering. Terry is a wash-out as a boxer and still, in his middle twenties, an errand boy for John Friendly. The man, as Brando plays him, has hidden complexities that only come to the surface through the half-articulate gropings in his conversations with Eddy and his brother Charlie. Terry's character seems to crystallize when he is put under pressure from both sides. The formation of Terry's individuality becomes apparent for the first time in the famous taxi scene with

Charlie. Although Terry is conscious of his duty to the underworld code of D and D (deaf and dumb), he finally begins to see his own worth as a person and understands that he must take a position of his own. His decision to talk to the Crime Commission is crucial to the outcome of the film, but it is only the denouement of Terry's long struggle to find out who he is.

How to Present *On the Waterfront*

On the Waterfront is a film that would benefit a great deal from a second showing to the film society audience. The picture often makes such a powerful first impression that it takes a second viewing to see both the strengths and weaknesses of the work as a whole.

Some suggested points of discussion on the film might be: try to enumerate the various ways in which the camera created or added to the story by color and composition (e.g. use of whites, grays and blacks; line, mass and balance), camera angles and movement, creation of atmosphere and mood. How was the music used during the film? What effect did it have? How does Kazan use realistic things like pigeons and Joey's jacket to help tell his story? (Note that pigeons are a constant object throughout the film; are they an important object? symbol?) How is the sound used creatively; for example, in the scene where Terry tells Eddy that he was involved in her brother's death? In trying to estimate the acting performances, be as detailed as possible in saying what made certain people stand out. What was the theme of the film? Were there traces of weakness in Kazan's direction, any slickness at the expense of depth, melodramatic touches that did not seem appropriate? Trace the development of Terry's self-awareness through its various stages of relationship with Charlie, John Friendly, Eddy, Father Barry. How is the individual choice the axis of the film? How does it illuminate the individual's dilemma in contemporary society?

IV. Ikiru

Japanese, 1952. Directed by Akira Kurosawa. Screenplay by Hideo Oguni, Shinobu Hashimoto and Kurosawa. Music by Fumio Yawoguchi. Photographed by Asaichi Nakai. Starring Takashi Shimura, Miki Odagiri, Yunosuke Ito and Nobuno Nakamura.

Background: Kurosawa and the Japanese Film

The birth of the Japanese film dates, in Western minds, from August, 1951, when Kurosawa's *Rashomon* was awarded the top prize at the Venice Film Festival. After this entrée, Japanese films became frequent festival winners: Kenji Mizoguchi's *The Life of O-Haru* (Venice, 1952) and *Ugetsu Monogatari* (Venice, 1953); Teinosuke Kinugasa's *Gate of Hell* (Cannes, 1954); Kurosawa's *Ikiru* (Stratford, 1960; Berlin, 1961) and *Yojimbo* (Best Actor, Venice, 1961). What amazed most people in the West was how suddenly and spectacularly Japan had made its entry into international competition. What many did not realize was that the ancestry of the Japanese film was almost as ancient as the venerable lines of the French and American cinema. At the time Kurosawa won his first prize in 1951, he had been a noted director in Japan for eight years while his older contemporary, Mizoguchi, had been directing some of Japan's most distinguished films since the early 1920's.

Rashomon became for many people the model of Japanese film making and the "period-film" par excellence; but such a judgment was neither accurate for the country's general production nor for the particular category of the period-film. A rudimentary knowledge of Japanese film history discloses a wide variety of film making that ranges from the modern comedy of manners to the political propaganda film. The period-film, like the American western, is a genre that spans the entire history of film making in the country; but it is by no means the only, nor even the typical, product of the industry. Just as it would be incorrect to classify something like *High Noon* simply as *the* classic western, so *Rashomon* cannot be called a typical period-film. Certain critics of the Japanese film have even said of *Rashomon* that "though classified as a period-film since it is set in the early Heian period, [it] is actually just about as far away from the standard Japanese period-film as one can get." [14]

Kurosawa himself has continued to experiment in each of his pictures so that it is difficult to put him into one category and regard him simply as a maker of historical period pieces. His career shows an amazing variety and virtuosity in the film medium. He made his debut as a director in 1943 with *Sanshiro Sugata*, a film of the Meiji period about the originator of Judo. Next he created a brilliant satire on the period-film itself called *Men Who Tread on the Tiger's Tail* (1945, withheld by both Japanese and occupation governments until 1953); and followed with *No Regrets for My Youth* (1946), a modern story about academic freedom; a part of a union propaganda film, *Those Who Make Tomorrow* (1946); and a modern love story à la Griffith in *Wonderful Sunday* (1947). In 1948 his film making reached maturity with *Drunken Angel*, a film ostensibly in the gangster genre but really an allegory on pessimistic postwar Japan. The hero of the film, an alcoholic doctor, is an em-

[14] Joseph Anderson and Donald Richie, *The Japanese Film: Art and Industry* (New York: Grove Press, 1960), p. 223.

bodiment of Kurosawa's fundamental optimism and
faith in the human spirit.

The Silent Duel, an unsuccessful melodrama about
venereal disease, was completed in 1949. This failure
was more than compensated for by his next film,
Stray Dog, which was an exciting detective story that
included the director's commentary on the social evils
of his time. The following year Kurosawa concentrated his criticism on the practice of irresponsible
journalism and turned out one of his least successful
films, *Scandal* (1950). Then came *Rashomon* (1950),
in which he returned to a period setting but incorporated a serious theme on the relativity of human truth.
In 1951 he turned to something he was later to repeat,
the adaptation of a Western literary classic. His version of *The Idiot,* however, was something less than
successful.

In 1952 Kurosawa completed what many consider
to be his masterpiece, *Ikiru* (translated as "to live"
or "living"). In it the director has combined the
humanism and social consciousness of his previous
films with a free-ranging experimentation in film technique that makes the film an exciting visual experience. Not satisfied with such an accomplishment, in
the following two years Kurosawa undertook a long
(three hours and twenty minutes) and expensive
period-film of epic proportions called *The Magnificent
Seven.* In 1955 he created an allegory about the people who live in a world under constant nuclear threat
called *I Live in Fear.* His treatment was on the level
of personal tragedy rather than mere politics like
many of the other Japanese bomb pictures of the decade. Four more recent films are all period-films of one
kind or other: *Throne of Blood* (1957, adaptation of
Macbeth), *The Lower Depths* (1958, adaptation from
Gorky), *Three Bad Men in a Hidden Forest* (1959)
and *Yojimbo* (1960). The most recent release in this

country is a detective film called *High and Low* (1963).

The Picture

Ikiru combines some of Kurosawa's most brilliant and varied film making techniques with a story that has several layers of meaning. In this confrontation with death, there is more than a personal drama of a man grasping for meaning in the last months of his life. There is trenchant social criticism that cuts across frontiers and nationalities to the heart of bureaucracy and stagnation wherever they exist.

Kurosawa invests his film with a strong sense of movement that has come to be one of the distinguishing marks of his pictures. There is, for example, a beaded curtain at the door of a bar that swings rhythmically in front of the camera; the tracking shot of the hero Mr. Watanabe as he moves along a crowded Tokyo street at night; the movement of a group of schoolchildren at a party in the background of a restaurant while a quiet, tense scene takes place in the foreground; finally, the gentle movement of a child's swing at the playground. All these uses of movement give an audience a strong kinesthetic experience that is so characteristic of movie art and, indeed, almost a Kurosawa trademark.

Rhythm is another important factor in *Ikiru*. Kurosawa, who has done most of his own editing, displays a sensitivity for the way in which his images flow across the screen. There is, for example, a contrast in tempo between the opening sequence (up to Watanabe's discovery that he has cancer) and the sequence in the night clubs. The scene in the bar where Watanabe meets the poet is long and almost monotonous in the slow rhythm of its editing, while the sequence in the night clubs which follows is a fantastic kaleidoscope of movement and frantic cutting. The rhythm

of the funeral banquet is leisurely and in keeping
with the gradual revelation of the hero's secret.

Kurosawa somehow manages to integrate the social
criticism and the personal tragedy of the film. Perhaps the best explanation of the film's unity is found
in the common solution that Kurosawa offers for both
the social and the personal problem: a form of humanism that is often found in his films. The director
has described this view of the world on one occasion
by saying: "If I look objectively at the pictures I
have made, I think I say: 'Why can't human beings
try to be happier?' *Living* (*Ikiru*) and *Record of a
Living Being* (*I Live in Fear*) are such pictures.
The Castle of the Spider's Web (*Throne of Blood*),
on the other hand, states why human beings must be
unhappy." [15]

Kurosawa's answer to the suffering of Mr. Watanabe and to the problem of the stifling bureaucracy
of city hall is, in fact, a kind of humanism. Watanabe,
faced with a death sentence, is forced out of his mum-
mified state to answer a fundamental question about
himself: not "Why must I die?" but "For what have
I been living?" Kurosawa answers the question by
saying that to live (*Ikiru*) is to love and to give one-
self for others. The bureaucracy in *Ikiru* may also
be seen as a failure by those in the government to
love and to understand that by their office they are
dedicated to working for others and not merely moving ahead in "the system". Until Watanabe gets beyond selfish love of his family and a narrow concern
for his position in city hall, he cannot face death. For
death, Kurosawa seems to be saying, is simply the
definitive end to life, not a reality in itself. Death
will have meaning only if that which has preceded it
contains an element of love, a going out to others.

---

[15] *Ibid.*, p. 380.

The first half of the film is a complex psychological development of a man who is faced with ending a life that does not have love and meaning. In the second part, Kurosawa gradually reveals by means of flashbacks the consequences of the hero's discovery of love. The final sequence illustrates the almost impossible human stagnation that bureaucracy generates. This stagnation seems to conquer Mr. Watanabe's idealistic friend in the office who, toward the close of the film, sinks slowly down behind a huge pile of official documents. Kurosawa's final view of the man, however, is of him looking at the playground that Watanabe built. This scene seems to confirm the basic belief that is behind all of Kurosawa's films and is at the heart of all reform: man's ability to achieve his humanity.

How to Present Ikiru

A little preparation and background would help an audience appreciate *Ikiru* more fully. It is a Japanese film and therefore strange for those who have seen few oriental films before. One thing worth noting is that the pace and rhythm of many Japanese films are much more leisurely and contemplative than these elements in American films. Some knowledge of the traditions of family relationships among the Japanese will make certain aspects of the story more clear. One must also recall the tremendous impact that Western civilization, especially a democratic form of government, has had upon the Japanese since World War II. The discussion leader should invite a person with a background and knowledge of the orient to be with the group and help discuss the film. If no one of this kind is available, the program note compiler should make a few helpful remarks in his notes on the film.

One practical point about the showing of the picture: the film is long and almost broken in two by Kurosawa's emphatic shift in story technique somewhat over half way through. If the film group is using only one projector some may get the idea that the film is finished if the reel break coincides with the end of Part I. It may happen (as it did at a large university showing) that the audience will get up and leave, thinking that the film is over. The group leader should warn the audience ahead of time.

The line of inquiry that the group might pursue in discussion would include some consideration of Kurosawa's technique. Besides this and some basic understanding of the Japanese background, the discussion might center around the choice that comes at the end of Part I. Many questions suggest themselves, but in case the inspiration of the discussion moderator and of the group should fail, here are some suggestions: trace the various stages of Watanabe's changing attitude toward death, the various psychological stages through which he passes. Discuss the hero's relationship with his son. Is Kurosawa critical of the traditional family ideals? How is Watanabe's decision at the restaurant the central action of the film, drawing both parts of the story together? What was the insight and the motivation behind the hero's new determination to live? Does the director manifest an attitude toward death in the film? How? If you have seen any other of Kurosawa's films, compare and contrast the treatment of the main character with that of Watanabe.

V. The Set-Up

American, 1949. Directed by Robert Wise. Produced by Richard Goldstone. Screenplay by Art Cohn, based on the narrative poem by Joseph Moncure March. Music by Constantin Bakaleinkoff. Photographed by Milton Krasner. Starring Robert Ryan,

Audrey Trotter, George Tobias, Alan Baxter and Wallace Ford.

Background: the American "Film Noir"

The Set-Up is a minor triumph in a kind of film making that died with the advent of television. The genre, called by French critics the *film noir*, was born in the early 1930's with Warner Brothers' *Little Caesar*. The gangster and crime film of the two decades that followed was a type of film that was at home on the regular-sized screen and seemed best to tell its story in simple black and white photography. These were the "gangster"movies as many Americans remember them, pictures without many big stars, emerging for the most part from the second feature units of Hollywood. Over a period of more than twenty years, the hundreds of film of this genre left behind a mountain of material for future sociologists and also an indelible mark on the history of the American film.

If the 1930's saw the birth of the *film noir* and its early nurturing with *Little Caesar, The Public Enemy* (1931) and *Scarface* (1932), there was a second stage of development that began in the early 1940's with John Huston's *The Maltese Falcon* (1941) and continued into the age of television. It is within this second tradition that *The Set-Up* must be placed. Following Huston's film and especially immediately after the war, there was a spate of *film noir* that created an atmosphere of violence that even the 1930's had not matched. One has only to recall some of the better known pictures of the decade immediately preceding *The Set-Up* to understand the kind of films that many American studios were producing. To mention only a few: *The Maltese Falcon; Murder, My Sweet; The Mask of Demetrios; The Big Sleep; The Lady from Shanghai; Dead Reckoning; Sorry, Wrong*

Number; Double Indemnity; Laura; The Postman Always Rings Twice; Rope; Sleep, My Love; The Killers; Crossfire; The Naked City; Nightmare Alley; The Kiss of Death; and *Thieves' Highway.* It was from a period of film making that produced motion pictures of this kind that *The Set-Up* came. The years immediately following the war were characterized by both a violence and a social concern that are to be found in Robert Wise's film.

The director of *The Set-Up,* Robert Wise, emerged from the Hollywood tradition, but his early career had been marked by two fortunate experiences that helped to lift him above many of the hacks who lived out their lives in the big studios. In 1940 Wise as a rising young editor for RKO was given the job of editing Orson Welles' first film, *Citizen Kane.* How much of the success of the film was due to Wise's skill no one can now say, but his association with Welles on this and his next film, *The Magnificent Ambersons,* gave the young editor a glimpse of what the film medium was capable of. From this experience, he moved on to another fortunate association. He became an editor for Val Lewton in the early stages of that producer's memorable series of horror films for RKO. At the beginning of 1944, he took over the direction of Lewton's *The Curse of the Cat People* midway through shooting and never returned to his job as editor.

Wise continued with Lewton for two more films, directing *Mademoiselle Fifi* and *The Body Snatchers* in 1944-45. Before making *The Set-Up* in 1949, he had experimented in the *film noir* with *A Game of Death* (1945), *Criminal Court* (1946) and *Born to Kill* (1947), besides broadening his experience with a western, *Blood on the Moon* (1948). When Wise came to make his film about boxing, he was a director with considerable background both as an editor and as a practitioner of the *film noir*. Such a background helps to explain the competence with which *The Set-Up* has been put together.

The Picture

The Set-Up is a boxing picture whose realism and brutality do not submerge but rather elevate the essential humanity of the central character, Stoker Thompson. The film is a trenchant indictment of professional boxing, especially in the lower circles of the sporting world. But it is the honesty of Robert Ryan's character of Stoker and the film's theme of humanity's survival in brutalizing situations that give continuing vitality to the film.

The endurance of *The Set-Up* as a tough piece of realism, however, is due not only to the acting and the story's theme but also in large measure to the very tight-knit structure of the film itself. A film script that originates from a short story often enjoys certain advantages of unity and concentration that one stemming from a novel does not have. *The Set-Up* is an adaptation of a narrative poem by J. M. March. There are no subplots, no superfluous parts, only one central action, Stoker's last fight and its consequences. There is no artificial telescoping of time in the story; it coincides exactly with the running time, 72 minutes. The locale is a run-down sports arena in a fictionalized American city, with its cheap hotel, bars, dirty streets and dark alleys. The unity of time, place and action helps to create a relentless tension that gives the film much of its impact.

Robert Wise makes telling use of his camera to communicate the setting of his story. His unobtrusive camera captures the oppressive atmosphere of the little second-story hotel room, the scabby dressing room, the dingy arena and the alley with its line of dustbins. The camera is there as a recorder, observing the *mise-en-scène,* creating an emotional resonance that helps to bring out the full meaning of the personal story of Stoker Thompson. Regardless of whether the film was shot on location or not, the surroundings as captured on the screen give the story the kind of setting that it needs.

Wise's editing is another important factor in the film's final success. During the long fight sequence, which takes almost a third of the film's running time, the director does two things at once: first, he captures the full ferocity and brutality of the fight itself by a series of close and medium camera placements; then he adds to this some commentative editing that forms a much more biting accusation of professional boxing than does the bruising action in the ring. By cutting to the crowd during the fight, Wise shows that the real savagery of the sport lies more with the crowd than with the boxers in the ring. He cuts from the fight to a woman who screams, "Kill him! Kill him!" as Stoker staggers under the pounding from his younger opponent. More than once the camera returns to a sadistic blind man who savors the frenzy of the crowd and delights in the details of Stoker's wounds.

The character of Stoker may seem too slight to merit great attention. In so brief a film where a third of the time is taken up with the fight itself, it is difficult to see much depth in this aging boxer. Of course, the same might be said of any character in a short story. Robert Ryan portrays the boxer with an underplayed intensity and low-keyed honesty that are right for the role. Stoker is no cardboard hero who rises to great heights to make virtue triumph. He is a thirty-five-year-old professional boxer who refuses to admit that he is finished, a man who seems afraid to quit. The very passivity of the character stands in contrast to any heroics, for Stoker is pictured as a man with his back to the wall: first with his wife who tries to force him to a decision to quit, then with another boxer in the ring, finally in the alley. He strikes and is struck; he evades but finally has to face himself. In choosing not to lie down, he wins much more than the fight. Stoker emerges as a human being, a small man, perhaps, but human in contrast to those around him.

How to Present The Set-Up

The Set-Up is placed fifth in the series because its extreme simplicity of structure as well as the somewhat obvious nature of the story might deceive an audience into paying slight attention to the film. It is a film, however, that demands a greater concentration and a keener awareness of technique in order to appreciate Wise's achievement. In showing the film, the projectionist should try to eliminate the reel break since a delay might tend to hurt the impact of the story more than one with a less tightly-knit structure.

The discussion leader could begin with questions on technique: if one were to remake the story today, would film or television do a better job with it? Try to enumerate the various ways in which Wise created the milieu of the story, the background against which the action is to be played. How has Wise's editing ability helped create a more closely-knit story in both the dressing room and the ring sequences? How are these two sequences contrasted in the type of editing they employ with the opening and closing sequence in the hotel room and the alley? What precisely was Wise's purpose in breaking up the bruising fight sequence with shots of the spectators? How many different camera positions can be recalled and what were the effects of these various positions in the film? In all of the questions of technique, the leader should ask how they were integrated into the story and how they helped to tell it.

Concerning content, one can pursue two paths: the film as a social document on the evils of professional boxing; or the personal story of Stoker Thompson. If the first topic is chosen for discussion, the group should be aware of the choice and not confuse the issue by switching back and forth. One may wish to examine the person of Stoker Thompson. Is there verisimilitude in this character? Is the motivation clear for his decision not to lie down? Is it mere anger at being betrayed by his manager? jealousy of the younger boxer? memory of his wife's pleas? or what? What makes Stoker stand out from the rest of the people in the story? Is the character of Julie believable? Explain how Stoker can be included as an example of the theme of the series.

VI. Diary of a Country Priest

French, 1951. Directed by Robert Bresson. Based on a novel by George Bernanos. Music by Jean-Jacques Grünenwald. Photographed by L. H. Burel. Starring Claude Laydu, Nicole Maurrey, Armand Guibert and Nicole Ladmiral.

Background: the Films of Robert Bresson

Robert Bresson is a director who is highly regarded by critics and other directors but one who has always been difficult for the general public. During his twenty years as a director he has made only six pictures: *Les Anges du Péché* (1943), *Angels of Sin,* unreleased in the United States, *The Women of Bois de Boulogne* (1945), *Diary of a Country Priest* (1951), *A Man Escaped* (1956), *Pickpocket* (1960) and *Procès de Jeanne D'Arc* (1963, unreleased in the United States). Because of the austerity of his method and the demands he makes upon his audience, Bresson, even when commercially distributed, has never had much box-office appeal.

All of Bresson's films reflect clearly the personal concern of the director for things of the spirit. His works share a vision of the invisible world of grace that Bresson has tried to manifest through the external world of material objects and surfaces, of phenomena like faces and hands. Henri Agel, the French critic, has said of Bresson's concern for spirit: "It is not in dramatic or psychological terms that Bresson's films are written; it is not a question of a narrative which tells of some everyday concrete things; nor is it a question of a character study which shows us persons that we can encounter on the streets. The action, the psychology is subordinated to a higher end, transcendent, oriented to a new dimension of the spiritual order."

The Picture

The Diary of a Country Priest is an adaptation of the novel by George Bernanos written in 1937. What Bresson has attempted to do in this screen version is to maintain the diary form, not simply to provide a framework for his sequences, but rather, it seems, to reveal little by little the spiritual struggle raging in the soul of the young curate. Consequently, the most important action of the story is not visible to the human nor the camera eye. However, Bresson saw in the diary form and the way he adapted it to the screen his best means of revealing this interior action.

In translating the novel into cinematic terms, Bresson has concentrated on close shots of the young priest's face. This constant use of the close-up of Claude Laydu indicates that for Bresson this is the best way by which the film medium can enter the invisible world of human emotion and reach the depths of the spirit. The critic Béla Balázs has made a great deal of the use that the silent films made of the close-up. He says that although the talking films have the opportunity of "explaining" the state of soul of a person, frequently "many profound emotional experiences can never be expressed in words at all." [16] Bresson has learned much from the silent films, it seems, especially from Dreyer's masterpiece, *The Passion of Joan of Arc*, where the use of close-up was dominant. Bresson's supposition seems clear: to penetrate the mystery of the human person, the camera must contemplate the human face.

The utter simplicity and lack of dramatic effect with which Bresson confronts the audience with the hero's face at various times and from different angles are the results of a style that is at once stark and poetic. One American critic complained that the non-professional actor playing the young priest has a face that is inexpressive and therefore boring. Such a remark shows that he did not appreciate what Bresson was trying to do. If it were merely a case of telling a sentimental story of an unsuccessful but sympathetic young curate, one might agree that Bresson has failed; he would have done better to have employed a well-trained and sensitive face like that of Pierre Fresnay (*Monsieur Vincent* and *God Needs Men*). But Bresson's interests lie deeper than mere psychology, as the critic Agel pointed out, and deal with the human spirit and its reaction to God's grace. In such a case the director has felt the need of a face of a man who is *not* acting. This desire for honesty at the expense of some of the "art" of performance may seem unimportant to those who do not share this approach to film making.

---

[16] Béla Balázs, *Theory of the Film* (London: Dennis Dobson Ltd., 1952), p. 65.

There are other techniques of the medium besides the close-up that should be noted in the film. The use of the written diary form is not a mere gimmick used to advance the story. The voice of the priest speaks while he writes the one or two sentences of each entry. This is done not to capsulize the coming action but to provide circumstances in which the priest's story can develop. These brief entries in the diary do not give the impression of constant flashbacks to a past time but rather a strong experience of the actuality of the present. When Bresson wants to reveal the interior disposition of the young priest, he will frequently use the actor's voice off-screen to let the audience know what he is thinking. Of course, this technique has been used to the point of triteness in many other films; but in *Diary of a Country Priest* Bresson has managed to transcend cliché with the honesty of his style.

Bresson's use of sound is important since his images are incapable of expressing the whole reality of his story. The use of the voice off-screen, the use of music to support and carry forward the emotion generated by the images, the natural sounds (the dog barking in the night, the tinkling of the sheep's bells, the heavy breathing of the young curate), the dialogue and prayers of the hero, even, as one critic observes, Bresson's use of silence to reveal the soul of the curé d'Ambricourt—all these point to the large measure in which sound helps to interpret the story of the country priest.

The concentration of the picture is entirely upon the figure of the young priest. He appears in all of the film's 35 scenes and only in the final shot of the cross (Bresson's ultimate simplification of his story to symbol) do we not have his physical presence. André Bazin, the late French critic, has compared this film to a passion play or to the stations of the cross. The

childlike young priest is led through physical suffering, misunderstanding, failure and calumny, even despair and death. His life is, indeed, a Christ-like *via
crucis* of humiliation and death. In many ways, however, the curé seems too passive, without enough
determination to take decisive action. Bernanos concludes his novel with the comment that "Grace is
everywhere. . ." This view of the reality of grace
should not destroy the individuality of the hero but
rather underscore it. Grace is at work in the spiritual
development of the curé d'Ambricourt; but it is the
personal commitment of faith, made and adhered to in
his spiritual struggle and agony, that forms the core
of the story. *The Diary of a Country Priest* tells the
story of interior action, the creation of a man of sor-
rows, a man who chooses and grows as a result of
that choice.

How to Present Diary of a Country Priest

This film has been placed last in the series for several reasons. First, Bresson's pictures are not easy
to understand; for they give the spectator a minimum
of help and call for a maximum of concentration. The
program notes should guide the audience's attention
to some of the important visual and aural images of
the film, but even for those of good will, the first viewing may be difficult.

If the discussion has taken the personal commitment of one of the characters in the film series as a
focal point of its study, then this film should be placed
last for a second reason. This is the story of a man
seeking God, one whose choice of faith is not made
clear to the audience because it is made long before
the film opens and only manifests itself indirectly in
the endurance and suffering of the young priest. This
is not the kind of choice nor the type of action that
audiences expect from a hero. However, the audience

may be in a better position to respond to this kind of film at the end of the series than it would before.

A major part of the discussion will probably center on content rather than on technique in this film. Questions that might be posed are: what film techniques help to tell the story? Why does Bresson use these particular ones? How does the atmosphere help to carry on the narrative? How does the music promote the story for the audience? What precisely is the commitment, the choice of the curé d'Ambricourt? How does the individual choice lie at the heart of the action in the film? What meaning does the remark of Dr. Delbend have when he says that he, the Abbé de Torcy and the young curate are all three similar in character? Delbend soon after commits suicide. Can one trace the passion theme throughout the film? What significance does the final sequence of the priest's death at the house of his former companion have for the rest of the story?

Appendix A

Hints on the Organization
of a Film Society

Government of the Society

When the purpose and the potential audience of
the society have been decided upon, it would be good
for the founding core to apportion to themselves the
various mechanical tasks involved in running an organization. Naturally appointment to office will be a
bit arbitrary at first, but once the society is functioning these offices will be decided upon by election of all
the members.

Officers necessary for operating a film society are:
a chairman who will function as general coordinator,
a business manager who will be in charge of finances
and bill paying, a secretary, a publicity manager and
an educational chairman who will be in charge of
compiling film notes, contacting speakers (if used by
the society) and leading the discussions. Some of
these jobs can be handled by only one person, but it is
not a good policy to overload the officers with too
much work lest enthusiasm begin to wane from the
outset.

The first duty of the secretary will be to contact
the various film distribution agencies to obtain catalogs of available films. (See list, page 150, for the
names of these agencies.) Do not restrict your film

sources only to companies dealing with feature films. Such sources as "The Educational Film Guide", "The Blue Book of 16mm Films", and the listing of films available from the local Public Library will provide invaluable material for obtaining short films to fill out your general program.

When the catalogs begin to arrive the officers should familiarize themselves with available films, the rental rates and the booking obligations. Information gained from these sources will figure importantly in future decisions. A word of caution: while reading these catalogs, you will find yourselves tending to be carried away as you discover the availability of movies you have long been eager to see. But remember, you do not have to see them all at once. The particular aim of your society should remain uppermost in your minds and should be the governing factor for film selection.

A final note: the Public Library, in addition to its film collection, will be valuable for its collection of books and periodicals on movies and allied topics. Knowledge of these holdings should be made available to all the officers and to the members of the society.

Now that you have an idea of the audience with which you plan to work and knowledge of the films available for your purposes, the next step will be to consider how you will finance the project.

Finances

Funds to finance your film society would seem to come either from outright subsidy by a school, church, club, or benefactor or will have to depend upon an admission charge of individual members. The source of funds will make some difference on film rental rates. For this information consult the rental scale found in the catalog of the particular agency with which you plan to deal.

No matter how you plan to finance the project you will have to expect to meet certain standard expenses. These expenses will vary in some measure according to particular circumstances, but in general they are: film rental and postage, rent for the room or auditorium where the films are to be shown and discussions held, projectionist's fee, advertising and ticket printing, film notes and certain miscellaneous expenses that crop up along the way.

If you plan to charge admission for the films, it is not a good idea to work in terms of individual performances. It is far better to issue membership tickets that cover the entire series. The reason for this should be obvious. If you charge for individual pictures, you may well end up in the red some time or another. A heavy snowstorm, for example, could lead to that awful experience of having an expensive movie on hand with no audience to pay for it. So for safety's sake it is much better to know where all the money is coming from to pay for the films you have contracted to show.

In addition to financial security for the society, the purchase of a series ticket has a good psychological effect upon the member. When a person buys his ticket, he commits himself to the entire series. This is important because you want to instill in the members' minds an attitude that belonging to this society is something more than merely going to see this or that movie that happens to strike their interest. A further practical point is that you can print the film titles and showing dates on the ticket which will serve the member as a ready source of reference.

When you are in the process of building membership, you may find it profitable to have a few tickets available for individual showings. This will give the opportunity to attract potential new members. The price of these tickets should be higher than that paid by series ticket holders. Thus, if the average cost per film for regular members is thirty cents, then the individual ticket should be fifty cents. This price difference will serve as an incentive to buy a series ticket. You may wish to continue this practice after the society has become well established since it will afford the regular members the chance to bring a guest to the showings and discussions. One word of caution: be sure not to issue more tickets for a particular showing than your seating capacity will allow.

Promotion

Do not think that you will automatically build up an interested membership simply because you have a program which you alone know is good. You must let the potential audience know that you have something for them that they will find not only interesting but of real value. Although you are not fundamentally in the movie exhibition business, still, while conducting the membership drive, you will have to function as promoters, publicists, copywriters, public speakers, and salesmen. And, when the society begins its showings, you will have to maintain a sense of showmanship lest the presentation become sloppy and amateurish.

Important as this sense of showmanship is, however, it is important that the atmosphere of honest study also be retained. The purpose of a film society is knowledge and appreciation; hence, a commercial element with its attendant spirit of the showman is only a means to achieve the primary aim of the society. In the following section devoted to the subject of location and projection, more specific and concrete illustrations will be given to enable you to give your showings a polished look.

Thus far activities have been largely restricted to work by and among the officers. You have established the special aims of your particular society, you have decided upon the films that will best achieve your purposes and you have focused upon that segment of the community from which to attract your members. Now you are ready to begin the actual membership campaign.

The publicity manager would do well to draw up a list of suggested outlets for the society's promotional material. If, for example, an audience is to be drawn from a particular group within a school—students of English, history or languages—then you will want to center attention on persons and places common to the particular group. It is wise to contact the members of the faculty to enlist their support. Interested teachers are of great value both by their actual membership in the society and in their talking up the value of the society to students and friends. Signs and/or brochures ought to be placed in areas particularly frequented by the students. In many schools, the various departments have special bulletin boards set aside for just this purpose. Further, you will want to find out if there is some particular publication read by the students. The school paper is a good outlet, but if the department has its own publication be sure to advertise there too. In short, the job of the publicity manager is to discover every possible means to draw to the attention of a target audience the aims and programs of the society.

An audience drawn from within a school or college campus is more easily contacted than one drawn from less restricted and less well-defined boundaries. Examples of areas of audience recruitment are church, business and professional groups. Perhaps the best method for drawing members from these loosely organized groups is to make contact with already existing organizations within the particular groups themselves. So, for example, you intend to build your society from persons already operative within a church structure; then the publicity manager will want to contact the officers of existing church organizations. He will, of course, make himself and the aims of the society known to the pastor. Once the pastor is convinced of the value of the society for his church, he may well be of assistance in promotion and in putting the facilities of the church building at your disposal. In this case the problem of finding a place to show the films and to hold discussions will be already solved.

Unless the business and professional groups are large enough to sustain membership for their own society, for example an aircraft plant or metropolitan hospital, your recruitment will have to come from combining members from several allied groups. You may well find it necessary to make this more universal approach in establishing a society within a church too. To make contact with business and professional groups, the publicity manager will want to deal with other organizations to which the potential film society member may already belong. Women's clubs, the P.T.A., business and professional organizations and the like will serve as excellent sources for names.

As you begin to enroll members into the society, these persons can be used as agents for contacting their friends and associates who would also be potential members. If you have made provision for single admissions, be sure to get the name of everyone who comes to these individual showings. Try to get the one-time viewer to become a series member. Do not be afraid to build up a large membership for the society. If the group gets too large for convenient discussion, it would be far better to break up into smaller groups for the purposes of discussion than to limit the size of the society as a whole. It goes without comment, that the more members you have the larger will be your income, and with the increased revenue you can obtain more films, more expensive films, and pay the cost of bringing in guest speakers. Group discussion is an important part of the society's activity and should not be sacrificed; therefore, you must use your imagination to find ways to have both a large membership and lively discussions.

Location and Projection

To assume a society will automatically succeed because you have a large membership — all of whom show a lively interest in the film program and discussion—is to court disaster. In an above section, it was noted that you need to maintain a sense of showmanship in your presentations lest what might have begun as an enthusiastic membership dwindle away to a select few who are willing to undergo any set of indignities to see a movie. The following comments on the mechanics of presentation may at first strike you as obvious and not worth mentioning. But more film societies have gone under because of sloppy and amateurish presentation than from lack of interest in the films or discussions.

In selecting a room or auditorium for your films and discussions, be sure that the size of the room is proportionate to the number of members in the society. While the difficulties of an overcrowded and cramped showing place are obvious, problems of too large a room are equally devastating. When a group spreads out all over a large room it is difficult for a speaker to make any necessary introductory remarks or carry on a profitable discussion. Further, it is bad psychology to give those present the impression that you were not able to attract enough persons to fill the room.

Other things to look for in addition to the size of the room are acoustics, since an audience will react quite strongly to a sound movie that cannot be heard; comfortable seating arrangement, for the seats should not only afford comfortable sitting, but should also be placed so that all can easily see the screen; and, lastly, adequate temperature control. Before each showing it is important always to check for proper ventilation. Further, the room should be able to be darkened so that the picture can be seen without distraction. If possible, it adds to a professional presentation of the movie to mask the bare 16mm screen and tripod combination by means of curtains or a simple wooden frame. This is a little thing, but it does much to remove the amateur stigma that so often surrounds the viewing of 16mm movies.

The projector and the film should be checked before each showing. Nothing gets the evening off to a worse start than mechanical difficulties in the projection of the picture. If there is no projection booth, then it is best to place the projectors above the heads of the audience, thus eliminating some of the distraction of the projector's noise.

The projectionist should know the machines and be able to make all the necessary minor adjustments that might occur in the course of the showing. Examples of such adjustments are: reframing the picture, adjusting the film loop, changing bulbs (light and sound) and cleaning dirt from the aperture.

If you plan to use two projectors for showings, there are several points to keep in mind. The projectionist must be able to interpret the cue signals indicating the end of the reel so he can smoothly switch over to the other machine. Whether you are using two projectors or not, it is important to avoid having the leaders of the film projected on the screen. Smooth changeovers from one projector to the other will naturally avoid this problem. If you are using only one projector, however, when the changeover cue appears on the screen turn off the projecting light and lower the sound. An audience will easily adjust to the necessity of changing reels, but they will not adjust to having their attention disrupted by the appearance of an end leader. When beginning another reel, start with the picture itself and not with the numbers on the head leader.

Finally, before each showing be sure to check the focus and sound level. The projectionist should be on the alert for these two points at all moments of the showing and not require comments from the audience before he makes the necessary adjustments.

Since the age and make of projectors will cause a difference in the quality of sound, shape of the picture and intensity of the light, every effort should be made to avoid glaring differences when the picture is switched from one projector to the other. If sound and picture quality is markedly different in the two machines you have at your disposal, you would be better advised to use only one machine. The moment it takes to change reels will be better received by an audience than will be the distracting difference between the two machines.

Always be sure the projector is in good working order. It would be far better to cancel a program than to present a sloppy showing or cause damage to the film print itself.

A final note: as the officers of the society you must not only present an attractive program and conduct stimulating discussions, you must also remember the obligation to provide for the physical comfort and welfare of the members.

Booking

By "booking" is understood the contract for a certain film or films to be shown by you on certain specified dates. Distribution companies have made this process as simple and expeditious as possible and anything peculiar to a particular agency is made quite clear in their catalog. The following comments are designed to give a general knowledge of booking procedure.

Booking should take place as far as possible in advance of desired show dates. Since most companies allow booking a year or more in advance, you would be well advised to take advantage of this long range booking in order to assure getting the desired movies on the show date you specify. Moreover, since many organizations are using films, you will often find yourself out of luck if you wait until a month before the desired show date. It is best to order films for a series one at a time. Indicate all the titles and show dates for the series. It does not matter that you are not booking all the films from the same agency. What is important is that you book all the films you wish to obtain from a particular company at the same time. Since most companies give a price reduction for series rentals, you save money and have the added assurance that all the films will be available when you want them.

If the series requires a particular order of presentation, indicate this fact. Sometimes a company will rearrange the order of films and show dates according to their availability. When such rearrangement will make a difference to a series, be sure to order well in advance and, if possible, give alternative titles. It is not always necessary to substitute, however, since you might be able to find the picture is available from another company.

When you have submitted your order, the company will send a confirmation of the booking. Be sure to check the titles and show dates indicated on the confirmation slip, because this represents your contract with the company. Titles and show dates listed on the confirmation slip are your reservations and will come as indicated. Therefore, any corrections must be made by you. Remember: the confirmation slip, not your original order, is the definite record of business between you and the company.

For safety and speed of delivery, be sure that the shipping instructions indicated at the time of booking include the name of the person, organization and address where you wish to have the film delivered. Generally, films will arrive two or three days before your show date. This will provide ample time to check the film to see that it has been rewound and is ready for projection. When a picture is shipped directly from the film company it will have been checked for any breakage, spliced where necessary and rewound for immediate projection. If the picture has been sent from some other film society showing, it is a good practice to check the film for any possible breakage or damage. This early arrival of the film will provide preview time to prepare any special notes or comments you might wish to have for the film. When you preview a film, always keep in mind that this is a special courtesy extended by the film distributor and is not to be considered an apportunity for an extra showing. Anytime you have an audience for your showings, no matter how small, you are expected to pay the distributors for their films.

Films should be returned no later than the day after your show date. The film distributing agencies will tell you how they want the films returned whether by mail or express. It is most important to follow all the shipping instructions. Sometimes it happens that you will be asked to ship the film directly to some other organization rather than to return it to the company. Any delay or mistake in shipping will result in great inconvenience for the next party. Common courtesy, then, requires that you read all shipping instructions and abide faithfully by them.

Payment for pictures varies somewhat from company to company. At the time of booking, make arrangements for the payment plan you wish to follow whether it be payment in advance, C.O.D. or the arranging of a charge account. If you plan to use the C.O.D. method, be sure to have sufficient funds available at the place of delivery to cover the rental and shipping charges.

Thus far we have been dealing with the mechanical aspects involved in forming and running a film society. The problems of physical location, projection and booking are similar to those met by anyone using motion pictures. It is in programming and presentation that the film society is distinctive. Here it is that creative forces are brought into play, and here it is that things become a bit more difficult.

The Program Director

We have discussed earlier (pp. 137 ff.) the general problems involved in programming and in presentation.

The following suggestions will treat of more specific and practical points that one beginning a film society will want to consider. It was pointed out above that programming for a society with a particular discussion goal will find film selection already directed by the topic, while the casual film society requires film selection be made among more commercially successful films. Since there are common mechanical elements of programming, it would be well to treat these points first and then look to the particular needs of a specific type of film society.

The burden for selecting programs belongs most

properly to the program director who will, of course, be assisted by the other members of the board. When the society has been functioning for some time, it is good to enlist the aid of the entire membership. But in the early stages of the society, the selection is best handled by the officers. You may find that this is the best way to program your series after you have become well established. This you will have to sense for yourselves as you go along. Since the success of your project depends greatly upon the quality of your programming, it is important that a person appointed to the task of program director have taste, common sense, some knowledge of films and an ability to know the feelings of the total membership.

The program director should first begin by reading through as many film catalogs as possible with an end in view of informing himself of what is available and the approximate costs involved. When he begins to draw up a potential list of titles, he should have his list contain two or three times more titles than actually required for the intended series. He must always be on guard to select those films which will be of interest to the general group and not merely to himself or some limited group.

When the list has been completed, he should show it to the officers and to any other persons who have experience and knowledge of the movies. He should add to his list any further suggestions his consultants might have.

The next step will be for the program director to meet with all the officers assembled together to discuss the various titles in terms of their suitability to the aims of the society. In addition to eliminating those titles which you find unsuitable to your aim, it is wise also to drop those pictures whose rental is beyond your present budget. It is far better to put off showing an expensive movie if it would mean having to sacrifice on the number or quality of shorts you will also want to include in your programs.

As the number of titles becomes more workable within the limits of the society, the next step to consider is the balance of pictures in terms of language and subject matter. If all the pictures selected are foreign, then it would be good to add a couple of English-speaking movies. If all the titles indicate serious subjects, then add two or three lighter pictures. Finally, if all the pictures are in black and white, then be sure to add at least one or two color movies.

Do not restrict discussion only to the selection of feature films; consider the shorter films that you will want to use to accompany the feature or to make up a single program of shorts.

You should now be in a position to select specific films for a series. At this time pair up the shorts with the features. This aspect of programming will require all your best talents in understanding the psychology of audiences. Serious features should be lightened with humorous shorts, dance or music shorts, or cartoons. A basic principle in successful programming is never overpower the audience with too heavy an evening of film fare; moderation and variety are the watchwords.

Finally, you will want to decide the order in which the films are to be presented. Unless a series is dictated by chronological development, try to get a variety between the old and the new, the serious and the funny, native and foreign. Be sure to choose a strong opener for the series and keep the springtime showings, if possible, a bit more on the lighter side. For showings on the college campus, keep in mind any special factors, such as exam tensions, that might unduly influence the reception of your program.

With these steps completed, you are now ready to print up the advertising and begin the appeal to attract members. If you are fortunate enough to have the budget supplied through some source other than subscription, you have nothing more to do after the booking and showing of the series than to sit back and wait for the compliments or complaints.

During the course of the series, the program director as well as the other officers should pay attention to the reactions of the audience in order to make any necessary adjustments in future programs. It is a good idea to keep a record of all the films you show with comments made concerning their reception so that future program directors will be able to avoid unnecessary mistakes.

When programming for the casual society, you will soon discover that within a group of this nature there will be an articulate core of "cinema addicts" who have particular pictures they want to see. This core is of value in your programming because of their interest and background knowledge, but they can also be a source of difficulty if you allow their enthusiasm to overly influence film selection. Often they are not interested in seeing the type of picture that will attract the mass audience. If you allow the programs to take an esoteric bent, then you will freeze out the casual filmgoers who, you will soon discover, make up the largest part of your membership income. If on the other hand, you select solely for the mass audience, you will lose the help of the articulate core. The task then becomes to please as many factions as possible so that you can keep up an interested, well-paying following.

It will be much easier to know the feelings of the study-type society since you will be engaging with them in discussion. The casual society is composed of much more fluid membership than the discussion group. These persons tend to drift from one organization to another and, in the case of campus societies, the members graduate and leave school. This rapid turnover is good in that you can repeat certain films more often than would be possible with the more stable membership. However, the casual members require a constant sales promotion to keep up their interest.

When selecting films for the casual society, the program director will want to pick his suggestions from among what are known as "the must see category". His choice of "must see" films will be directed along the same avenue of thinking as that employed by the commercial theater owner whose prime motive is financial profit. Top-ten lists, oscars and film festival prizes will be the usual sources.

When programming for a group whose interest is in an organized approach to understanding artistic and social values of motion pictures, the officers will want to be sure that the topic chosen for the projected series meets with the approval of their potential members. It is more important to have a common understanding concerning the aim of the series than it is in the case of the casual society. Membership in the study society is attracted more by the subject to be treated than it is by particular film titles. It is very important, then, that the officers be in close contact with potential members so they will know the specific needs and desires of the group. For it is only through understanding between those who will organize the series and those who will participate in the discussions that interest and enthusiasm can be developed.

Some Important Addresses

1. Film Sources: more important sources are marked with an asterisk [*], the letters in [ ] following the names are the code used in Appendix C.

American Art and History
Films
41 West 47th Street
New York 36, N. Y.

Athena Films
570 Seventh Avenue
New York 36, N. Y.

*Brandon Films, Inc. [B]
200 West 57th Street
New York 19, N. Y.

Film Center, Inc.
20 East Huron Street
Chicago 11, Illinois

Western Cinema Guild,
Inc.
381 Bush Street
San Francisco 4, Calif.

British Information Services
% Contemporary Films
267 West 25th Street
New York 1, N. Y.

Center for Mass Communications
Columbia University Press
1125 Amsterdam Avenue
New York 25, N. Y.

*Cinema Guild [IFC]
10 Fiske Place
Mount Vernon, N. Y.

Audio Film Classics
2138 East 75th Street
Chicago 49, Illinois

Audio Film Classics
406 Clement Street
San Francisco 18, Calif.

Cinema 16 [C 16]
175 Lexington Avenue
New York 16, N. Y.

*Contemporary Films, Inc.
[C]
267 West 25th Street
New York 1, N. Y.

*Continental 16 [Con 16]
6 East 39th Street
New York 16, N. Y.

Dominant Pictures Corpora-
tion [DP]
247 Park Avenue
New York 17, N. Y.
[Warner Bros. Features]

Encyclopedia Britannica Films
1150 Wilmette Avenue
Wilmette, Illinois

Film Classic Exchange [FCE]
1926 S. Vermont Avenue
Los Angeles 7, Calif.

Film Images
1860 Broadway
New York 23, N. Y.

*Films, Incorporated [FI]
1150 Wilmette Avenue
Wilmette, Illinois

Ideal Pictures [IP]
58 E. South Water Street
Chicago 1, Illinois

International Film Bureau
332 South Michigan Avenue
Chicago 4, Illinois

*Janus Films, Inc. [J]
267 West 25th Street
New York 1, N. Y.

Janus Film Library
514 Davis Street
Evanston, Illinois

Maya Deren
35 Morton Street
New York 14, N. Y.

*Museum of Modern Art
Film Library [MMA]
11West 53rd Street
New York 19, N. Y.

Pictura Films
41 Union Square West
New York 3, N. Y.

Rembrandt Films
267 West 25th Street
New York 1, N. Y.

Trans-World Films, Inc.
[TWF]
53 W. Jackson Blvd.
Rm 530
Chicago 4, Illinois

United World Films
Government Division
1445 Park Avenue
New York 29, N. Y.

Walt Disney Productions
16mm Division
350 South Buena Vista
Burbank, Calif.

Canadian Federation of Film
Societies
1762 Carling Avenue
Ottawa 3, Ontario
Canada

Centre Catholique de Radio,
Cinéma et Télévision
315 Rue de Montigny, Est
Montreal 18, P. Q.
Canada

The Chicago Center for Film
Study [program notes
available]
[Division of Catholic Adult
Education Center]
21 West Superior Street
Chicago, Illinois 60610

Educational Film Library
Association
250 West 57th Street
New York 19, N. Y.

George Eastman House
900 East Avenue
Rochester, N. Y.
[large private film archive]

Gotham Book Mart
41 West 47th Street
New York 36, N. Y.

2. Other Addresses for Information

American Federation of Film
Societies
144 Bleecker Street
New York 12, N. Y.

Art Film Publications
[program notes available]
Box 19652
Los Angeles 19, Calif.

British Film Institute
81 Dean Street
London, W. 1
England

Larry Edmonds Bookshop
6658 Hollywood Blvd.
Hollywood 28, Calif.

National Legion of Decency
453 Madison Avenue
New York 22, N. Y.

O.C.I.C. Secretariat General
[International Catholic
Office of the Film]
8 Rue de l'Orme
Brussels 4
Belgium

Program Note Exchange of
  AFFS
Dartmouth Film Society
P. O. Box 831
Hanover, N. H.

Robert Flaherty Foundation
RFD #1
Brattleboro, Vermont

St. Clement's Film Ass'n.
[program notes available]
423 West 46th Street
New York, N. Y.

Appendix B
A Survey of Film Societies[1]

The following survey of film societies is included here as an appendix in order to provide those who are beginning their own film groups with an idea of the policies and practices of other societies. The information does not pretend to be statistically valid for generalizing about all film societies in the country; rather it is an informational survey of what a small number of representative film societies are doing at the time of the survey (completed January, 1964). In the opinion of the authors, presently existing film society practices do not always represent the ideal; but they are a necessary base from which one must work in attempting to improve film education.

Much of the information may not be relevant for those who have had experience in film society work. A complete summary of the results is presented for the sake of those who may be new to the work of running a film society. The summary follows the pattern of the questionnaire that formed the base of the survey.

I. General Information

Respondents: 55 of the 91, or about 60% of the questionnaires were answered; of these 55 there were 52 with active programs. The 52 groups that make up the group surveyed represent a fair cross section of film societies throughout the country, being divided

---

[1] This survey appeared under a slightly different form as a chapter in James L. Limbacher's (ed.) *The American Film Society Handbook.*

among societies connected with colleges and universities (26), independent groups (16) and societies affiliated with public libraries, museums or cultural centers (10). These societies, for the most part (38), are members of the American Federation of Film Societies, a non-profit organization whose purpose is "to encourage the higher development of film as a form of art and education" by a number of informational and service activities (address in Appendix A).

There was a great range in the sizes of the various societies, from the 28 member Salisbury Film Society of Salisbury, Conn., to the 1,500 member Los Alamos Film Society. But numbers alone do not seem to be an index of success, for the Salisbury Film Society has been an active group since its foundation in 1951. Generally the university film groups have a larger membership (e.g. Purdue, 1,200; MIT, 1,200; Wichita, 800; University of California, Santa Barbara, 700; UCLA, 450; Dartmouth, 350). The problem of the university societies is not so much attracting numbers as keeping the balance in a group that has an almost complete turnover in membership every four years.

Finally, it seems that for the groups included in the survey 16mm is still the universally accepted way to show film society programs; 39 societies used 16mm exclusively, 10 used both 16mm and 35mm, and only one used 35mm exclusively.

II. Structure of the Film Societies

Programming: Programming is the most crucial factor in any film society as Chapter III pointed out above. The questionnaire made several inquiries about the policy of programming among the current societies. In answer to the first question about *how* the program was chosen, the respondents indicated three

common methods: an individual selected the program
for the group (18), a committee made the selection
(26), or the entire membership voted on the program (10).

Another question that was asked was whether the
society ever sponsored specialized programs; for instance, a series on the German silent films, a Bergman
series, or the films of Garbo, and so forth. There
were 24 groups who had sponsored such programs and
even a few who made such specialized series a policy
of their group. For example, Roosevelt University
Film Society has a policy of showing only specialized
series; these programs have included in recent years:
"U. S. Films of Early Sound" (Spring, 1963), "Eastern European Films" (Winter, 1963), "Hollywood
Stars of the 1920's" (Fall, 1962). Dartmouth College
Film Society has a large yearly program that in 1963-
64 featured the following: a series of 14 films from
the *Sight and Sound* top-ten survey (e.g. *Citizen Kane,
Intolerance, Ivan the Terrible I* and *II, La Terra
Trema*); an Ozu retrospective of 5 films; a UFA
retrospective of 10 German sound films; the complete
work of John Huston (to *Freud*). Delta Kappa Alpha
of UCLA has been responsible for such series as "The
French New Wave" (1958), "Films of Orson Welles"
(1960), "Shakespeare on Film" (1962) and "Pictures by Stanley Kramer" (1963). The University of
Illinois Film Society interspersed a series of 3 to 6
films among the offerings of their annual series of
about 15 films and thus combined the concentration
of a specialized program with the variety needed to
attract a large audience; some of their programs included 6 films on themes of war, 3 films of Garbo, 5
films of social comment, 6 films of Hitchcock, Huston
and Dovzhenko. Finally, Wichita and Boston universities supplemented their regular programs with special film festivals, setting aside a few days to view and

discuss the films of Eisenstein, Cocteau and contemporary Poland.

The non-specialized or general interest program will usually include certain classic films that everyone should have seen once or twice. A list of 933 different films was compiled from program listings submitted by the participants in the survey. These films had been shown within the last four years, though a few programs extended back somewhat farther. The following list of 77 titles are of those films that were among the most popular among the 50 groups submitting sample programs. Most of them are worthy of consideration by the programmer who is faced with the problem of selecting titles for a varied program.

77 Most Frequently Shown Films

1. M (20 times)
2. Chaplin (an evening of his short comedies) (15)
3. Citizen Kane (15)
4. Potemkin (13)
5. La Strada (13)
6. The General (12)
7. Pather Panchali (12)
8. Rashomon (12)
9. Ugetsu (12)
10. L'Atlante (11)
11. Birth of a Nation (11)
12. Intolerance (11)
13. Olympia I (11)
14. Seventh Seal (11)
15. Magnificent Seven (Seven Samurai) (11)
16. Aparijito (10)
17. Bicycle Thief (10)
18. Carnival in Flanders (10)
19. Olympia II (10)
20. Umberto D (10)
21. Forbidden Games (9)
22. Henry V (9)
23. Hiroshima Mon Amour (9)
24. Italian Straw Hat (9)
25. Ivan the Terrible I (9)
26. Le Million (9)
27. Miss Julie (9)
28. Passion of Joan of Arc (9)
29. Sawdust and Tinsel (9)
30. Alexander Nevsky (8)
31. 400 Blows (8)
32. Gate of Hell (8)
33. The Great Adventure (8)
34. Ikiru (8)
35. Nights of Cabiria (8)
36. Vampyre (8)
37. I Vitelloni (8)
38. World of Apu (8)
39. Young and the Damned (8)
40. A Nous la Liberté (7)
41. Ballad of a Soldier (7)
42. Cabinet of Dr. Caligari (7)
43. Genevieve (7)
44. Grand Hotel (7)
45. Grand Illusion (7)
46. Miracle of Milan (7)

47. Phantom of the Opera (7)
48. Zero for Conduct (7)
49. Captain from Coepenick (6)
50. Chien Andalou (6)
51. Diabolique (6)
52. La Dolce Vita (6)
53. Duck Soup (6)
54. Earth (6)
55. Les Enfants Terribles (6)
56. Fall of the House of Usher (short) (6)
57. Greed (6)
58. The Kitchen (6)
59. The Last Bridge (6)
60. The Love Game (6)
61. Loves of Jeanne Ney (6)
62. Louisiana Story (doc) (6)
63. Magnificent Ambersons (6)
64. Momma Don't Allow (short) (6)
65. Nanook of the North (doc) (6)
66. Night at the Opera (6)
67. Night Mail (doc) (6)
68. Night of the Hunter (6)
69. Orpheus (6)
70. Open City (6)
71. The Quiet One (doc) (6)
72. Rules of the Game (6)
73. Sunrise (6)
74. Thirty-Nine Steps (6)
75. Viridiana (6)
76. White Mane (short) (6)
77. The White Sheik (6)

Program Notes: There is little to add about program notes; 49 of the 52 groups made use of program notes though the quality and purpose of the program notes varied widely. Some consisted in nothing more than a quickly typed ditto of a few snatches of the first review of the film that came to hand or even the notice from the film catalog. Other program notes were competent analyses that included background material and film credits and were obviously compiled for a serious film audience. Sources for program notes listed by respondents were AFFS Program Note Exchange, British Film Institute, film catalogs, newspaper and magazine reviews, film journals and books.

Financing: To the questions of how the society was financed and what was done with any surplus money there were a number of answers. One might summarize the methods of financing the film society in the order of their relative popularity (and success?): subscription of season membership; subscription plus single admission; college, museum or public library budget; donations solicited from individual benefactors; advertising in program notes.

In the few cases where there was a surplus, the money was disposed of in the following ways: helping to finance next year's program; sponsoring a bonus film for the present season; buying better equipment; . returning surplus to sponsoring institution; donating to the Museum of Modern Art Film Library; buying books and films for society library; sponsoring lectures; donating to scholarship funds for young film makers.

Lecture and Discussion: Very few of the societies had any regular program of lectures and of the few who had them at all (15) most only had them about once a year.

The discussion fared somewhat better although even here there were only 22 of the 51 groups who had tried to conduct discussion sessions. Of these 22, there were many fewer who seem to have had any continuing success with the idea. Some reasons for the difficulties were: only the well-informed are capable and interested and they will discuss among themselves; to organize discussion tends to put constraints on people's spontaneity and kills lively interchange; discussion immediately following the film does not give people a chance to absorb and reflect upon what they have seen.

Some of the objections seem specious and some are genuine difficulties, but the real problem often lies with the very concept of the film society itself. If its purpose is clearly conceived to promote genuine education in appreciation and judgment of motion pictures, then discussion should become one of the most valuable means of accomplishing this end, as the section in Chapter III points out.

III. Conclusion

There can be no universally valid conclusions from this survey. It is hoped that those who read it will realize that though film societies do not exist in an ideal order, there are a number who have succeeded in promoting genuine appreciation and education among their audiences. The means used are the careful selection of programs, well prepared program notes, occasional lectures and well organized discussions. The survey has shown that the goals of a film society can be accomplished if its foundations are laid on the solid base of clear objectives, dedication and hard work.

Appendix C

The Specialized Program

The advantages of the specialized program have been discussed in Chapter III. This appendix includes a number of suggestions for various kinds of film series with a brief sampling of titles. The sources where the films are available are listed in brackets following the titles and may be found in Appendix A. These titles are only suggestive and do not exhaust the possibilities for the series under which they are listed; nor do the series here outlined exhaust the possibilities for imaginative specialized programming. It is hoped that these suggestions will stimulate ideas of program committees whose task it is to choose the program best suited for their particular audience.

I. Historical Development of the Film Medium 1895-1964

This is an area of great importance but one so broad that it includes all films. No better suggestion can be made than that the program committee examine the series offered by the Museum of Modern Art Film Library.

II. Film Type

The type or genre has been suggested in chapters III and IV of this book. The ones listed here are only a few of the possibilities.

1. *The Western: An American Myth*

The Covered Wagon (1923) [IFC] [1]

---

[1] IFC: Cinema Guild: International Film Classics (see Appendix A).

> *The Iron Horse* (1924) [FI]
> *Tumbleweed* (1925) [IFC]
> *Stagecoach* (1939) [C, FI]
> *The Gunfighter* (1950) [FI]
> *Shane* (1953) [FI]
> *One-Eyed Jacks* (1961) [FI]

2. *Film Noir: Crime and Police, USA*

> *Little Caesar* (1930) [B]
> *The Public Enemy* (1931) [B]
> *The Maltese Falcon* (1941) [B, C, FI]
> *The Big Sleep* (1946) [B]
> *The Kiss of Death* (1947) [FI]
> *Thieves' Highway* (1949) [FI]

3. *Documentary: Reality through the Camera Eye:*
Consult the Museum of Modern Art Film Library catalog of documentary films. Since most documentaries
are not full length pictures, they might be scheduled with
an appropriate feature film or made into an evening's
program by combining several.

> *Nanook of the North* (1922) [B, C]
> *Granton Trawler* (1934) [C]
> *Man of Aran* (1934, full length) [B, C]
> *The River* (1937) [B, C]
> *Diary for Timothy* (1945) [C]
> *The Exiles* (1961, full length) [C]

4. *Experimental: New Frontiers:* Like the documentary, the experimental film is not generally full
length and so should be scheduled with a feature film
or several experimentals together. Cinema 16 has the
largest holding in this area.

> *Entr'Acte* (1924) [MMA]
> *Menilmontant* (1925) [MMA]
> *Meshes of the Afternoon* (1943) [C16, MMA]

> *Fiddle de dee* (1947) [C16]
> *The Blood of Beasts* (1949) [C16]
> *Between Two Worlds* (1940) [C16]

5. *The American Musical*

> *The Love Parade* (1929) [MMA]
> *Top Hat* (1935) [FI]
> *Meet Me in St. Louis* (1944) [FI]
> *Singin' in the Rain* (1952) [FI]
> *Lili* (1953) [FI]
> *The King and I* (1956) [FI]

6. *American Humor on the Screen: Comedy:* Chaplin is available from many sources. A few have been listed under his name in the section on directors at the end of this appendix.

> *When Comedy Was King* (compilation film on comedy) [FI]
> *Long Pants* (1927) [MMA] Harry Langdon
> *The General* (1926) [MMA] Buster Keaton
> *A Haunting We Will Go* (1939) [FI] Laurel and Hardy
> *A Night at the Opera* (1935) [FI] The Marx Brothers
> *The Bank Dick* (1940) [C] W. C. Fields

III. Nationalities

There are a number of ways to program films from various countries. A few countries have been treated more thoroughly to give the reader an idea of what might be done. Similar series should be worked out for other countries.

1. *American:* consult the American directors listed at the end of this appendix.

2. *French*

    (A) *Beginnings of French Sound Film:*

          1930-40

        A Nous la Liberté (1931) [C]
        La Maternelle (1933) [MMA]
        Zéro de Conduite (1933) [B]
        Carnival in Flanders (1936) [B]
        Rules of the Game (1939) [C, J]

    (B) *From the War to the New Wave:*

          1941-1958

        The Devil's Envoys (1942) [B]
        Beauty and the Beast (1946) [B]
        Symphonie Pastorale (1946) [TWF]
        Orpheus (1950) [B]
        We Are All Murderers (1952) [B]
        Forbidden Games (1952) [IFC]

    (C) *New Wave: 1959-*

        The Hole (1959) [Consort/Orion]
        Breathless (1959) [B]
        400 Blows (1959) [IFC]
        Hiroshima Mon Amour (1959) [IFC]
        The Cousins (1959) [B]
        Cleo from 5 to 7 (1961) [IFC]

3. *German:* consult the Museum of Modern Art Film Library catalog. Also see what Siegfried Kracauer has on the German film from 1919-1933 in his book, *From Caligari to Hitler.*

4. *Japanese:* consult directors Kurosawa and Mitzoguchi in directors' section; also the collection of Japanese films held by Brandon Films, Inc.

5. *Italian:* consult directors Antonioni, De Sica, Fellini, Rosellini and Visconti.

Neo-realism in Italy: 1942-?

Open City (1945) [B]
Mafia (1948) [B]
La Terra Trema (1948) [   ]
Without Pity (1948) [B]
The Bicycle Thief (1949) [B]
Umberto D (1951) [IFC]

6. *Swedish:* consult Bergman under directors; also the Museum of Modern Art Film Library catalog for older films.

7. *Spanish:* see under Buñuel for directors; Mexico, Spain, Argentina and other Spanish-speaking countries have produced films of merit that should be studied.

8. *Russian*

(A) *Three Russian Masters: Eisenstein, Pudovkin, Dovzhenko 1924-1930*

Strike (1924) [B]
Potemkin (1925) [B]
Mother (1926) [B]
End of St. Petersburg (1927) [B]
Storm Over Asia (1928) [B]
Arsenal (1929) [B]
The General Line (1929) [B]

(B) *Since Sound in the USSR: 1931-1963*

Road to Life (1931) [B]
The Childhood of Maxim Gorky (1938) [B]
Ivan the Terrible, I and II (1944, 1946) [B]
The Forty First (1956) [B]
The Lady with the Dog (1960) [B]
My Name Is Ivan (1963) [B]

IV. The Stars

1. *The Great Personalities of the '20's*

> Hart: *Tumbleweed* (1925) [IFC]
> Chaplin: see under directors
> Pickford: *New York Hat* (1912 short) [IFC]
> > *The Gaucho* (1927) [MMA]
> Fairbanks: *The Mark of Zoro* (1920) [MMA]
> Valentino: *Son of the Sheik* (1926) [IFC]
> Chaney: *The Phantom of the Opera* (1925) [IFC]
> The Gishes: *Orphans of the Storm* (1922) [MMA]

2. *Stars of the American Sound Film:* besides the two listed, one could select twenty more stars for series; for example, Brando, Monroe, Gable, Laughton, Muni and so forth.

(A) *Garbo*

> *Anna Christie* (1930) [, FI]
> *Grand Hotel* (1932) [B]
> *Queen Christiana* (1933) [B, FI]
> *Anna Karenina* (1935) [FI]
> *Camille* (1936) [B, FI]
> *Ninotchka* (1939) [FI]

(B) *Bogart*

> *The Petrified Forest* (1936) [B]
> *The Maltese Falcon* (1941) [B]
> *Casablanca* (1942) [B]
> *The Big Sleep* (1946) [B]
> *Treasure of the Sierra Madre* (1948) [B, FI]
> *The Caine Mutiny* (1955) [IFC]

V. Literature and the Cinema

1. *Shakespeare on Film*

> *Henry V* (1944) [C]
> *Hamlet* (1948) [C]
> *Macbeth* (1948) [B]
> *Julius Caesar* (1953) [FI]
> *Richard III* (1955) [B]
> *Romeo and Juliet* (1956) [C]

2. *Novels into Film:* this series follows the pattern suggested by George Bluestone in his book, *Novels into Film,* and might make a good core for a college class on the topic of film adaptation of literary sources.

> *The Informer* (1935) [B, C, FI]
> *Wuthering Heights* (1939) [   ]
> *Pride and Prejudice* (1939) [FI]
> *The Grapes of Wrath* (1940) [B, C, FI]
> *The Ox-Bow Incident* (1943) [B, FI]
> *Madame Bovary* (1949) [FI]

N.B. Many other novels could be substituted for one or other of the above. The Dickens' novels, for example, might form a series, or great French novels like *Les Miserables, The Red and the Black, Gervaise (L'Assommoir)* and so forth.

VI. Themes

The advantage and importance of a series built around a common theme have been discussed elsewhere and a complete analysis of a theme program given in Chapter IV. A series of this kind will vary a great deal, depending on the age, background and particular interests of an audience. The five themes listed below will give some idea of the possibilities of this approach; but this type of program counts to an even greater extent upon the imagination of the program committee than the other series suggested in this section.

1. *Youth in Revolt*

> *Shoeshine* (1946) [B]
> *The Blackboard Jungle* (1954) [FI]
> *Rebel Without a Cause* (1955) [FI]
> *East of Eden* (1955) [FI]
> *400 Blows* (1959) [IFC]
> *The Loneliness of the Long Distance Runner* (1961) [Con 16]

2. *Prejudice*

> *They Won't Forget* (1937) [B]
> *Professor Mamlock* (1938) [B]
> *Crossfire* (1947) [B, FI]
> *Gentleman's Agreement* (1947) [B, FI]
> *Intruder in the Dust* (1949) [B, FI]
> *The Lawless* (1950) [B]

3. *The Successful American*

> *Citizen Kane* (1941) [B, FI]
> *Executive Suite* (1954) [FI]
> *The Man in the Gray Flannel Suit* (1955) [FI]
> *Patterns* (1956) [IFC]
> *A Face in the Crowd* (1957) [FI]
> *Sweet Smell of Success* (1957) [IFC]

4. *Problems of Peace and War:* Consult Robert Hughes' (ed.) book, *Film: Book 2: Films of Peace and War,* for some discussions and opinions of various film makers on the subject.

> *The Man I Killed* (1932) [MMA]
> *The Battle of San Pietro* (1944) [MMA]
> *Neighbors* (1952) [C16 short]

Children of Hiroshima (1952) [B]
I Live in Fear (1955) [B]
The Burmese Harp (1956) [B]
Hiroshima Mon Amour (1959) [IFC]

5. *Man Faces God*

The Passion of Joan of Arc (1928) [MMA]
Day of Wrath (1940) [MMA]
God Needs Men (1950) [B]
Diary of a Country Priest (1951) [B]
The Burmese Harp (1956) [B]
Winter Light (1962) [J]

VII. Directors

The purpose of devoting such a large section to film directors has several reasons behind it. It is the director who, in the last analysis, is the chief creator of a film and it is to him that the serious student of the medium must turn for careful and prolonged study. On a more practical level, this section is primarily meant to provide program committees of film societies with information for selecting films; it will also provide a convenient reference to the work of thirty distinguished directors. It should be carefully noted, however, that this catalog is primarily a working list and not a definitive recording of each director's films. For exhaustive and detailed lists of the work of these men, the reader is referred to studies of the individual director in books and film journals like *Sight and Sound* and *Films in Review*.

Only a limited number of sources of rental have been consulted (those listed in Appendix A); therefore, if no source is listed for a particular film, it does not necessarily mean that it is not available.

The reader will immediately notice the absence of most of the younger directors from this appendix. This is not an oversight nor a prejudice against contemporary film makers. The list is primarily a practical source for film society directors and not simply a reference tool. Consequently only those directors were listed who have a fairly representative number of films to their credit and whose films are generally available from 16mm sources in this country.

There are important older directors who might have been listed here but were not. Choice and its consequences are the prerogative and burden of the chooser. So it is throughout this appendix. It was impossible to include more than the thirty who were selected. For those who wish to find other listings, they should consult: Georges Sadoul's *Histoire du cinéma mondial* (Paris: 1959), pp. 523-56; Penelope Houston's more modern list in *The Contemporary Cinema* (Pelican: 1963), pp. 197-206; and Andrew Sarris' check list of some American directors in *Film Culture* 28 (Spring, 1963), pp. 1-68.

ANTONIONI, Michelangelo. (Ital.) 1912-

1942-47: *Gente del Po* (doc.); 1948: *N.U.* (doc.) [C16]; 1949: *L'Amorosa Menzagna* (doc.); 1950: *La Villa dei Mostri* (doc.); *Cronica di un Amore*; 1952: *I Vinti*; 1953: *La Signora senza Camilie*; "Tentato Suicido" (a section of *Love in the City*) [B]; 1955: *Le Amiche*; 1957: *Il Grido (The Outcry)* [C]; 1960: *L'Avventura* [J]; 1960: *La Notte*; 1961: *The Eclipse*; 1964: *The Red Desert*.

BERGMAN, Ingmar. (Swedish) 1918-

Screenplays: 1944: *Torment* (directed by Alf Sjorberg) [J]; 1947: *Woman Without a Face* (directed by G. Molander); 1948: *Eva* (directed by G. Molander); 1950: *While the City Sleeps* (directed by L-E. Kjellgren); 1951: *Divorced* (directed by G. Molander); 1956: *The Last Couple Out* (directed by Alf Sjorberg).

Films directed by Bergman: 1945: *Crisis*; 1946: *It Rains on Our Love*; 1947: *A Ship to India*; *Night is My Future*; 1948: *Port of Call* [J]; *The Devil's Wanton* [IFC]; 1949: *Three Strange Loves* [J]; *To Joy*; 1950: *This Can't Happen Here*; *Illicit Interlude* (British title *Summer Interlude*) [J]; 1952: *Secrets of Women* [J]; *Monika* (British title *Summer with Monika*) [J]; 1953: *The Naked Night* (British title *Sawdust and Tinsel*) [B]; 1954: *A Lesson in Love* [J]; 1955: *Dreams* (British title *Journey into Autumn* [J]; *Smiles of a Summer Night* [J]; 1956: *The Seventh Seal* [J]; 1957: *Wild Strawberries* [J]; *Brink of Life* [IFC]; 1958: *The Magician* [J]; 1959: *The Virgin Spring* [J]; 1960: *The Devil's Eye* [J]; 1961: *Through a Glass Darkly* [J]; 1962: *Winter Light* [J]; 1963: *The Silence*; 1964: *Not to Speak about All These Women*.

BRESSON, Robert. (French) 1907-

1934: *Les Affaires Publiques* (short); 1943: *Les Anges du Péché*; 1944: *Les Dames du Bois de Boulogne* [B]; 1951: *Diary of a Country Priest* [B]; 1956: *A Man Escaped* [C]; 1960: *Pickpocket* [C16]; 1962: *Procès de Jeanne d'Arc*.

BUNUEL, Luis. (Span.) 1900-

1928: *Un Chien Andalou* [MMA]; 1930: *L'Age d'Or*; 1932: *Las Hurdes* (*Land without Bread*); 1947: *Gran Casino*; 1949: *El Gran Calavera*; 1950: *The Young and the Damned* (*Los Olvidados*) [B]; *Susana*; 1951: *La Hija del Engaño*; *Una Mujer sin Amor*; *Subida al Cielo* [TWF]; 1952: *El Bruto*; *Adventures of Robinson Crusoe* [Twy] [2] *El* (*This Strange Passion*) [B]; 1953: *Abismos de Pasion* (*Wuthering*

---

[2] Twy: Twyman Films, Inc., 329 Salem Ave., Dayton 1, Ohio.

Heights); *La Ilusión Viaja en Tranvía*; 1954: *El Rio y la Muerte*; 1955: *Celà s'Appelle l'Aurore*; *Ensayo de Un Crimen*; 1956: *La Mort en ce Jardin*; 1958: *Nazarin*; 1959: *La Fièvre Monte à El Pao*; 1960: *The Young One (La Jeune Fille)*; 1961: *Viridiana* [IFC]; 1962: *The Destroying Angel*; 1964: *Le Journal d'une Femme de Chambre*.

CAPRA, Frank. (USA) 1897-

1926: *The Strong Man*; 1927: *Long Pants* [MMA]; *For the Love of Mike*; 1928: *That Certain Feeling*; *So This Is Love*; *The Matinee Idol*; *The Way of the Strong*; *Say It With Sables*; *Submarine*; *Power of the Press*; 1929: *Younger Generation*; *Donovan Affair*; *Flight*; 1930: *Ladies of Leisure*; *Rain or Shine*; 1931: *Dirigible*; *Miracle Woman*; *Platinum Blonde*; 1932: *Forbidden*; *American Madness*; 1933: *Bitter Tea of General Yen*; *Lady for a Day*; 1934: *It Happened One Night*; *Broadway Bill*; 1936: *Mr. Deeds Goes to Town* [B]; 1937: *Lost Horizon* [B]; 1938: *You Can't Take It With You* [B]; 1939: *Mr. Smith Goes to Washington* [B]; 1941: *Meet John Doe* [FI]; 1944: *Arsenic and Old Lace* [B, FI]; 1942-45: Capra worked on the *Why We Fight* series of war documentaries for U. S. government; 1946: *It's a Wonderful Life*; 1948: *State of the Union*; 1950: *Riding High*; 1951: *Here Comes the Groom* [FI]; 1959: *A Hole in the Head*; 1961: *A Pocketful of Miracles*.

CHAPLIN, Charles S. (USA) 1889-

1914: Chaplin did 35 short comedies for Keystone: *Making a Living* [MMA, IFC]; *Kid Auto Races at Venice*; *Mabel's Strange Predicament*; *Between Showers* [B, IFC]; *A Film Johnnie* [IFC]; *Tango Tangles*; *His Favorite Pastime*; *Cruel, Cruel Love*; *The Star*

Boarder; Mabel at the Wheel; Twenty Minutes of Love; Caught in a Cabaret [C, IFC]; *Caught in the Rain; A Busy Day; The Fatal Mallet; Her Friend the Bandit; The Knockout* [IFC, MMA]; *Mabel's Busy Day; Mabel's Married Life; Laughing Gas* [B, IFC]; *The Property Man* [IFC]; *The Face on the Barroom Floor* [B, IFC]; *Recreation; The Masquerader* [B, IFC, MMA]; *His New Profession; The Rounders* [B, IFC, MMA]; *The New Janitors; Those Love Pangs* [IFC]; *Dough and Dynamite* [C, IFC]; *Gentlemen of Nerve* [B]; *His Musical Career; His Trysting Place* [C, IFC]; *Tillie's Punctured Romance* [B, C, FI]; *Getting Acquainted* [MMA]; *His Prehistoric Past.* 1915: Chaplin wrote and directed a dozen shorts for Essanay: *His New Job* [FCE]; *A Night Out* [IFC]; *The Champion* [IFC]; *In the Park* [C, IFC]; *The Jitney Elopement* [FCE]; *The Tramp* [IFC, MMA, MSP][3]; *By the Sea; Work* [IFC]; *A Woman* [MMA]; *The Bank* [C, MMA]; *Shanghaied; A Night in the Show* [IFC]. 1916-17: Chaplin made 14 films for Mutual: *Carmen* [MSP]; *Police* [IFC, MMA]; *The Floorwalker* [C, IFC]; *The Fireman* [C, IFC]; *The Vagabond* [C, IFC]; *One A.M.* [C, IFC]; *The Count* [C, IFC]; *The Pawnshop* [IFC]; *Behind the Screen* [C, IFC]; *The Rink* [C, IFC]; *Easy Street* [C, IFC]; *The Cure* [C, C16, IFC]; *The Immigrant* [C, C16, IFC]; *The Adventurer* [C, IFC]. 1918: Chaplin was with First National: *Triple Trouble* [IFC]; *A Dog's Life; The Bond* [IFC]; *Shoulder Arms;* 1919: *Sunnyside; A Day's Pleasure;* 1920: *The Kid;* 1921: *The Idle Class;* 1922: *Pay Day;* 1923: *The Pilgrim; A Woman of Paris;* 1925: *The Gold Rush;* 1928: *The Circus;* 1931: *City Lights;* 1936: *Modern Times;*

---

[3] MSP: Modern Sound Pictures, 1410 Howard St., Omaha 2, Neb.

1940: *The Great Dictator;* 1947: *Monsieur Verdoux;* 1952: *Limelight;* 1957: *A King in New York.*

CLAIR, René. (French) 1898-
(Pseudonym for Renè Chomette)

1924: *Paris qui Dort; Entr'Acte* [MMA]; 1925: *La Fantome du Moulin Rouge; Le Voyage Imaginaire;* 1926: *Le Proie du Vent;* 1927: *The Italian Straw Hat* [C]; 1928: *Les Deux Timides;* 1930: *Under the Roofs of Paris* [B]; 1931: *Le Million* [MMA]; 1932: *A Nous la Liberté* [C]; 1933: *14 Juliette;* 1935: *Le Dernier Milliardaire;* 1938: *The Ghost Goes West* [B, C]; *Break the News;* 1941: *The Flame of New Orleans;* 1942: *I Married a Witch* [C]; 1944: *It Happened Tomorrow;* 1945; *And Then There Were None;* 1947; *Le Silence est d'Or;* 1950: *Beauty and the Devil* [B]; 1952: *Beauties of the Night* [B]; 1955: *Les Grandes Manoeuvres;* 1957: *Gates of Paris (Portes des Lilas)* [B]; 1960: "The Marriage" in *Three Fables of Love* [J].

CLEMENT, René. (French) 1913-

1938: *Soigne ton Gauche;* 1942; *Ceux du Rail* (doc); 1943: *La Grande Pastorale* (doc); 1946: *La Bataille du Rail; Le Père Tranquille; Beauty and the Beast (with Cocteau)* [B]; 1947: *Les Maudits;* 1949; *The Walls of Malapaga (Au delà les Grilles)* [B]; 1952: *Forbidden Games* [IFC]; 1954: *Lovers, Happy Lovers;* 1956: *Gervaise;* 1958: *This Angry Age;* 1960: *Purple Noon;* 1961: *Che Gioia Vivere;* 1963: *Le Jour et l'Heure.*

DE SICA, Vittorio (Ital.) 1902-

1939: *Rose Scarlatte;* 1940: *Madalena; Zero in Condotta;* 1941: *Teresa Venerdi; Un Garbaldino al Convento;* 1942: *The Children Are Watching Us* [B];

1946: *La Porta del Cielo; Shoeshine* [B?]; 1949: *Bicycle Thief* [B]; 1951: *The Miracle of Milan* [IFC?]; 1952: *Umberto D* [IFC]; 1953: *Statzione Termini;* 1955: *Gold of Naples* [B]; 1956: *The Roof* [B]; 1961: *Two Women* [IFC]; 1963: *The Condemned of Altona;* 1964: *Yesterday, Today and Tomorrow.*

EISENSTEIN, Sergei M. (USSR) 1898-1948.

1924: *Strike* [B]; 1925: *Potemkin* [B]; 1928: *Ten Days That Shook the World* (also known as *October*) [B]; 1929: *The General Line* (also known as *Old and New*) [B]; 1938: *Alexander Nevsky* [B]; 1939: *Time in the Sun* (produced by Marie Seton from footage by Eisenstein for his unfinished *Que Viva Mexico!*) [B]; 1944: *Ivan the Terrible*, Part I [B]; 1946: *Ivan the Terrible*, Part II [B].

FELLINI, Federico (Ital.) 1920-

Fellini wrote scripts for many Italian directors from 1943 on: *e.g.* 1947: Bonnard's *Campo de Fiori;* Lattuda's *Without Pity;* 1948: Germi's *Mafia;* for Rossellini he did: 1945: *Open City;* 1946: *Paisan;* 1948: *The Miracle;* 1951: *Europa 51.*

Direction: 1950: *Footlights* (*Luci del Varietà*); 1952: *The White Sheik* [J]; 1953: "Love Cheerfully Arranged" as part of *Love in the City* [B]; *I Vitelloni* [J]; 1954: *La Strada* [B]; 1955: *Il Bidone* (*The Swindle*) [IFC]; 1957: *Nights of Cabiria* [B]; 1960: *La Dolce Vita* [IFC]; 1961: "The Dream of Dr. Antonio" as part of *Boccaccio 70;* 1963: *8½.*

FLAHERTY, Robert J. (USA) 1884-1951.

1920-22: *Nanook of the North* [B, IFC, MMA]; 1923-5: *Moana* [MMA]; 1925: *Story of a Potter; The Twenty-Four Dollar Island;* 1926-7: *White Shad-*

ows of the South Seas (Flaherty did the scenario but did not finish out the picture and it remains unsigned); 1928-31: *Tabu;* 1932: *Industrial Britain* [MMA]; 1932-34: *Man of Aran* [B, C]; 1935-37: *Elephant Boy* (Flaherty worked with A. Korda on the film); 1939-42: *The Land* [MMA]; 1948: *The Louisiana Story* [C].

FORD, JOHN (USA) 1895-

1917: *Cactus, My Pal; Joan of the Cattle Land; The Cattle War; The Round Up; The Range War; The Trail of Shadows; The Secret; The Scrapper; The Soul Herder; Straight Shooting; The Secret Man; Bucking Broadway;* 1918: *Phantom Riders; The Hill Billy; Wild Women; Thieves' Gold; The Scarlet Drop; Hell Bent; A Woman's Fool; Three Mounted Men;* 1919: *Roped; A Fight for Love; Bare Fists; Riders of Vengeance; The Outcasts of Poker Flat; Ace of the Saddle; Rider of the Law; A Gun Fightin' Gentleman; Marked Men.* 1920: *The Prince of Avenue A; The Girl in Number 29; Hitchin' Posts; Just Pals;* 1921: *The Big Punch, The Freeze Out; The Wallop; Desperate Trails; Action; Sure Fire; Jackie;* 1922: *Little Miss Smiles; Silver Wings; The Village Blacksmith;* 1923: *The Face on the Bar-Room Floor; Three Jumps Ahead; Cameo Kirby;* 1924: *Hoodman Blind; North of Hudson Bay; The Iron Horse* [MMA, FI]; *Hearts of Oak;* 1925: *Lightnin', Kentucky Pride; The Fighting Heart; Thank You;* 1926: *The Shamrock Handicap; The Blue Eagle; Three Bad Men;* 1927: *Upstream; Mother Machree;* 1928: *Four Sons; Hangman's House; Napolean's Barber; Riley, the Cop;* 1929: *Strong Boy; Black Watch; Salute;* 1930: *Men Without Women; Born Reckless; Up the River;* 1931: *The Seas Beneath; The Brat; Arrowsmith;* 1932: *Air Mail; Flesh;* 1933: *Pilgrimage; Doctor Bull;* 1934: *The Lost Patrol; The World Moves On; Judge Priest;*

1935: *The Whole Town's Talking; The Informer* [B, C, FI]; *Steam Boat Around the Bend;* 1936: *Prisoner of Shark Island* [FI]; *Mary of Scotland* [FI, B]; *The Plough and the Stars;* 1937: *Wee Willie Winkle; Hurricane;* 1938: *Four Men and a Prayer; Submarine Patrol;* 1939; *Stagecoach* [C, CG, FI, TWF]; *Young Mr. Lincoln; Drums Along the Mohawk* [FI]; 1940: *The Grapes of Wrath* [B, C, FI, MMA]; *The Long Voyage Home* [B, C, FI, TWF]; 1941: *Tobacco Road* [B, FI]; *How Green Was My Valley* [B, FI]; 1942: *The Battle of Midway* (doc.); 1943: *We Sail at Midnight;* 1945: *They Were Expendable* [FI]; 1946: *My Darling Clementine* [B, FI, MMA]; 1947: *The Fugitive* [FI]; 1948: *Fort Apache* [FI]; *Three Godfathers* [FI]; 1949: *She Wore a Yellow Ribbon* [FI, MSP, TWF]; 1950: *When Willie Comes Marching Home* [FI]; *Wagonmaster* [FI, MSP]; *Rio Grande* [FI]; 1951: *This Is Korea* (doc.); 1952: *What Price Glory; The Quiet Man* [FI]; 1953: *Mogambo* [FI]; 1954: *The Sun Shines Bright* [AFC][4]; 1955: *The Long Grey Line* [AFC, B, MSP]; Mr. Roberts (with M. LeRoy) [FI]; 1956: *The Searchers* [FI]; 1957: *The Wings of Eagles* [FI]; *The Rising of the Moon;* 1958: *The Last Hurrah* [AFC, B, C]; 1959: *Gideon of Scotland Yard* [B, TWF]; *The Horse Soldiers;* 1960: *Sergeant Rutledge;* 1961: *Two Rode Together;* 1962: *The Man who Shot Liberty Valance* [FI]; 1963: *Donovan's Reef;* 1964: *Cheyenne Autumn.*

GRIFFITH, David Wark (USA)   1875-1948.

Partial list 1908-1914: *i.e.* those films of this period that are available for rental: 1907: *Rescued from an Eagle's Nest* (acted in by Griffith, directed by Porter) [MMA]; 1908: *At the Crossroads of Life* (acted by

---

[4] Audio Film Classics (*cf.* Cinema Guild, Appendix A).

Griffith, directed by Wallace McCutcheon) [MMA];
1909: *A Son's Return* [IFC]; *The Lonely Villa*
[MMA]; *1776 or The Hessian Renegades* [MMA];
1911: *The Lonedale Operator* [MMA]; 1912: *The
Musketeers of Pig Alley* [MMA]; *The New York Hat*
[IFC]; 1913: *Broken Ways* [IFC]; *Judith and Bethu-
lia* [IFC]; 1914: *The Avenging Conscience* [MMA];
The Mother and the Law [MMA]; *Home Sweet Home*
[MMA]; 1915: *Birth of a Nation* [IFC, MMA];
1916: *Intolerance* [MMA]; 1918: *Hearts of the
World*; *The Great Love*; *The Greatest Thing in Life*;
1919: *A Romance of Happy Valley*; *The Girl Who
Stayed at Home*; *Broken Blossoms* [MMA]; *True
Heart Susie* [MMA]; *The Fall of Babylon*; *Scarlet
Days*; *The Mother and the Law*; *The Greatest Ques-
tion*; 1920: *The Idol Dancer* [MMA]; *The Love
Flower*; *Way Down East* [MMA]; 1921: *Dream
Street*; 1922: *Orphans of the Storm* [MMA]; *One
Exciting Night*; 1923: *The White Rose*; 1924: *Amer-
ica* [MMA]; *Isn't Life Wonderful* [MMA]; 1925:
Sally of the Sawdust; *That Royale Girl*; 1926: *Sor-
rows of Satan*; 1928: *Drums of Love*; *Battle of the
Sexes*; 1929: *Lady of the Pavements*; 1930: *Abraham
Lincoln*; 1931: *The Struggle*.

HAWKS, Howard (USA) 1896-

1926: *The Road to Glory*; *Fig Leaves*; 1927: *The
Cradle Snatchers*; *Paid to Love*; 1928: *A Girl in
Every Port*; *Fazil*; *The Air Circus*; 1929: *Trent's
Last Case*; 1930: *The Dawn Patrol* [DP]; 1931: *The
Criminal Code*; 1932: *The Crowd Roars* [DP];
Scarface; *Tiger Shark*; 1933: *Today We Live*; 1934:
Twentieth Century [IFC]; *Viva Villa* (signed by Jack
Conway); 1935: *Barbary Coast*; 1936: *Ceiling Zero*;
The Road to Glory [FI]; *Come and Get It* (with
William Wyler); 1938: *Bringing Up Baby* [FI];

1939: *Only Angels Have Wings;* 1940: *His Girl Friday;* 1941: *Sergeant York* [B, DP, FI]; *Ball of Fire;* 1943: *Air Force;* 1944: *To Have and Have Not* [B, DP]; 1946: *The Big Sleep* [B]; 1948: *Red River; A Song Is Born;* 1949: *I Was A Male War Bride* [FI]; 1952: *The Big Sky* [B, FI]; *Monkey Business* [FI]; "Ransom of Red Chief" of *O'Henry's Full House* [FI]; 1953: *Gentlemen Prefer Blondes* [FI]; 1955: *The Land of the Pharaohs;* 1959: *Rio Bravo;* 1962: *Hatari!* 1964: *Man's Favorite Sport.*

HITCHCOCK, Alfred (G.B., U.S.A.) 1899-

1925: *The Pleasure Garden* [IFC]; 1926: *The Mountain Eagle; The Lodger* [MMA]; 1927: *Downhill; Easy Virtue; The Ring;* 1928: *The Farmer's Wife; Champagne; The Manxman;* 1929: *Blackmail* [MMA]; 1930: *Juno and the Paycock; Elstree Calling; Murder;* 1931: *The Skin Game;* 1932: *East of Shanghai; Number Seventeen; Rich and Strange;* 1933: *Waltzes from Vienna;* 1934: *The Man Who Knew Too Much;* 1935: *The 39 Steps;* 1936: *Secret Agent;* 1937: *Sabotage;* 1938; *The Lady Vanishes; A Girl Was Young;* 1939: *Jamaica Inn;* 1940: *Rebecca* (first Hollywood picture) [B]; *Foreign Correspondent* [C, FI]; 1941: *Mr. and Mrs. Smith; Before the Fact; Suspicion* [B, FI]; 1942: *Saboteur;* 1943: *Shadow of a Doubt;* 1944: *Lifeboat* [FI]; 1945: *Spellbound* [B]; 1946: *Notorious* [B]; 1947: *The Paradine Case* [B]; 1948: *Rope;* 1949: *Under Capricorn;* 1950: *Stage Fright;* 1951: *Strangers on a Train;* 1952: *I Confess;* 1954: *Dial M for Murder; Rear Window;* 1955: *To Catch a Thief* [FI]; *The Trouble with Harry* [FI]; 1956: *The Man Who Knew Too Much* (remake of 1934 film) [FI]; *The Wrong Man* [FI]; 1958: *Vertigo* [FI]; 1959: *North by Northwest* [FI]; 1960: *Psycho* [FI]; 1963: *The Birds;* 1964: *Marnie.*

HUSTON, John (USA) 1906-

Screenplays[5]: 1938: *The Amazing Dr. Clitterhouse* [DP]; *Jezebel*; 1940: *Dr. Erhlich's Magic Bullet* [FI]; 1941: *High Sierra* [DP]; *Sergeant York* [B, FI]; 1946: *Three Strangers*.

Direction: 1941: *The Maltese Falcon* (also wrote screenplay) [B, C, FI, TWF]; 1942: *In This Our Life* (also wrote screenplay); *Across The Pacific* [FI, DP]; *Report from the Aleutians* [MMA]; 1944: *The Battle of San Pietro* [MMA]; 1945: *Let There Be Light* (not released by U. S. Gov't); 1947: *The Treasure of the Sierra Madre* [B, C, FI, TWF]; 1948: *Key Largo* [B, TWF]; 1949: *We Were Strangers*; 1950: *The Asphalt Jungle* [B, FI]; 1951: *The Red Badge of Courage* [B, FI]; 1952: *The African Queen*; *Moulin Rouge*; 1953: *Beat the Devil*; 1956: *Moby Dick*; 1957: *Heaven Knows, Mr. Allison* [FI]; 1958: *The Barbarian and the Geisha* [FI]; *The Roots of Heaven* [FI]; 1960: *The Unforgiven*; 1961: *The Misfits*; 1962: *Freud*; 1963: *The List of Adrian Messenger*; 1964: *Night of the Iguana*.

KUROSAWA, Akira (Japan) 1910-

(N.B. Japanese titles are not generally given)

1943: *Sanshiro Sugata*; 1945: *Men Who Tread on the Tiger's Tail* [B]; 1946: *No Regrets for My Youth*; *Those Who Make Tomorrow*; 1947: *Wonderful Sunday*; 1948: *Drunken Angel* [B]; 1949: *The Silent Duel*; *Stray Dog*; 1950: *Scandal*; *Rashomon* [IFC] (possibly a third one in 1950: *Mata Au Himade: Jusq'à notre prochaine Rencontre*); 1951: *The Idiot*; *Escape at Dawn* (*Evasion à l'Aube*); 1952: *Ikiru* (*To Live*) [B]; 1954: *The Seven Samurai* [IFC]; 1955: *I Live in Fear* [B]; 1957: *Throne of Blood* [B];

---

[5] Other screenplays: *Murders in the Rue Morgue*; *Law and Order*; *A House Divided*.

1958: *The Lower Depths*; *Three Bad Men in a Hidden Forest* (*Kakushitoride No San Aksunin*); 1960: *Yojimbo*; 1962: *The Bad Sleep Well*; 1963: *High and Low*.

LANG, Fritz (Ger., USA) 1890-

1919: *Halb Blut*; 1920: *Die Spinnen*; *Hara Kiri* (Madame Butterfly); 1921: *Der Müde Tod* (*Destiny*) [MMA]; 1922: *Dr. Mabuse, Gambler* (Dr. Mabuse der Spieler); 1924: *The Nibelungen* (*Siegfried Kriemhild's Revenge*) [B]; 1927: *Metropolis* [B]; 1928: *The Spys* (*Spione*) [MMA]; 1929: *The Woman in the Moon* (*Die Frau im Mond*) [B]; 1931: *M* [IFC]; 1933: *The Testament of Dr. Mabuse* (*Das Testament des Dr. Mabuse*); *Liliom*; 1936: *Fury* [B, FI]; 1937: *You Only Live Once* [C]; 1938: *You and Me*; 1940: *The Return of Frank James* [FI]; 1941: *Western Union* [FI]; *Man Hunt* [FI]; 1942: *Hangmen Also Die* [C]; 1943: *The Ministry of Fear*; 1944: *Woman in the Window*; 1945: *Scarlet Street*; 1947: *Cloak and Daggers*; 1948: *The Secret Beyond the Door* [B]; 1950: *American Guerillas in the Philippines* [FI]; 1952: *Clash by Night*; 1953: *Blue Gardenia*; 1954: *Human Desire*; 1955: *Moon Fleet* [FI]; 1956: *While the City Sleeps*; 1957: *Beyond the Reasonable Doubt*; 1958: *The Indian Tomb*; 1960: *The Thousand Eyes of Dr. Mabuse*.

LEAN, David (Brit.) 1908-

1942: *In Which We Serve* (with Noel Coward); *This Happy Breed*; 1943: *Blithe Spirit*; 1945: *Brief Encounter* [C]; 1946: *Great Expectations* [C]; 1947: *Oliver Twist*; 1950: *One Woman's Story*; *Madaleine*; 1952: *Breaking the Sound Barrier* [IFC]; 1954: *Hobson's Choice*; 1955: *Summertime*; 1957: *Bridge on the River Kwai*; 1962: *Lawrence of Arabia*.

MIZOGUCHI, Kenji (Japan) 1898-1956.

Selected films: 1924: *Foggy Harbor*; 1925: *Street Sketches (Gaijo no Suketchi)*; 1926: *A Paper Doll's Whisper of Spring (Kami-Ningyo Haru no Sasayaki)*; 1928: *Passion of a Woman Teacher (Kyorne no Onna Shisho)*; 1929: *Tokyo March*; *Metropolitan Symphony (Tokai Kokyogaku)*; *Hometown (Furusato)*; 1931: *And Yet They Go On (Shinkamo Karera wa Iku)*; *The Dawn of the Founding of Manchuko and Mongolia*; 1932: *Timely Mediator (Toki no Ujigami)*; 1933: *White Threads of the Cascades*; 1935: *Sisters of the Gion (Gion Shimai)*; 1936: *Osaka Elegy (Naniwa Eriji)*; *The Gorge between Love and Hate (Aienkejo)*; 1937: *Ah, My Hometown (Aa Furusato)*; 1939: *The Story of the Last Chrysanthemum (Zangiku Monogatari)*; 1940: *Woman of Osaka (Naniwa Onna)*; 1941: *The Life of an Artist (Geido Ichidai Otoko)*; *The Loyal 47 Ronin*; 1944: *Three Generations of Danjuro (Danjuro San-dai)*; 1946: *Utamaro and his Five Women (Utamaro o Meguru Go-min no Onna)*; *Women's Victory (Josei no Shori)*; 1947: *The Love of Actress Sumako (Joyu Sumako no Koi)*; 1948: *Women of the Night (Yoru no Onnatachi)* [B]; 1950: *Picture of Madame Yuki (Yuki Fujin Ezu)*; 1951: *Life of Madame Musashino (Musashino Fujin)*; 1952: *The Life of O-Haru (Saikaku Ichidai Onna)*; *Ugetsu Monogatari* [IFC]; 1953: *Gion Music (Gion Bayashi,* remake of the 1935 film); 1954: *The Broken Woman (Umasa No Onna)*; *A Story from Chikamatsu (Chikamatsu Monogatari)*; *Sansho the Bailiff (Sansho Dayu)* [B]; 1955: *The Princess Yang (Yokihi)*; *The New Tales of the Taira Clan (Shin Heike Monogatari)*; 1956: *Street of Shame (Akasen Chitai)* [IFC].

PUDOVKIN, V. I. (USSR) 1893-1953.

1925: *Chess Fever* (comic short co-directed by P.);

1926: *Mother* [B]; 1925-26: *The Mechanics of the Brain* (documentary) [B]; 1927: *The End of St. Petersburg* [B]; 1928: *Storm Over Asia* [B]; 1932: *The Story of a Simple Case*; *Life is Very Good*; 1933: *Deserter*; 1938: *Mother and Son*; *Victory*; 1939: *Minin and Pozarsky*; 1940: *20 Years of Cinema* (co-directed by P. and Esther Shub); *Suvorov* (co-directed by P. and M. Doller); 1941: *Feast at Zhirmunka* (2 reel war film); 1943: *In the Name of the Fatherland*; 1946: *Admiral Nakhimov*; 1948: *Three Meetings* (contribution by P. to film biographies of scientists); 1950: *Zhukovsky*; 1953: *The Return of Vasily Bortnikov* [B].

RAY, Satyajit (India) 1921-

1952-5: *Pather Panchali* [IFC]; 1956: *Aparajito* [IFC]; 1957: *The Philosopher's Stone*; 1958: *The Music Room* (*Jalsaghar*); *The World of Apu* [B]; 1960: *Devi* [IFC]; 1961: *Two Daughters* (*Teen Kanya*); *Tagore* (doc.) [C]; 1962: *Kanchenjungha*; *Abhijan.*

RENOIR, Jean (French) 1894-

1924: *La Fille de l'Eau*; 1926: *Nana*; 1927: *Charleston, Marquita*; 1928: *La Petite Marchande d'Alumettes*; 1929: *Tire-au-Flanc*; *Le Tournoi*; *Le Bled*; 1931: *On Purge Bébé*; *La Chienne*; 1932: *La Nuit du Carrefour*; 1933: *Chotard et Cie*; *Madame Bovary*; 1935: *The Crime of Monsieur Lange* [B]; *Toni*; 1936: *La Vie est à Nous*; *Les Bas-Fonds*; 1936-46: *A Day in the Country* (*Une Partie de Campagne*) [C]; 1937: *Grand Illusion*; *La Marseillaise*; 1938: *La Bete Humaine*; 1939: *Rules of the Game* (*La Règle du Jeu*) [C]; 1941: *Swamp Water*; 1943: *This Land is Mine* [FI]; 1944: *Salute to France* [MMA]; 1945: *The Southerner* [B, C, FI]; 1946: *The Diary of a Chamber-

maid; 1947: *The Woman on the Beach*; 1951: *The River*; 1952: *The Golden Coach* (*Le Carrosse d'or*) [B]; 1955: *French Cancan*; 1956: *Eléna et les Hommes*; 1959: *Picnic on the Grass* [C]; *Le Testament du Docteur Cordelier*; 1962: *The Elusive Corporal* (*Le Caporal épinglé*).

ROSSELLINI, Roberto (Italian) 1906-

1938: Scenarist for *Luciano Serra Pilota*; 1941: collaborated with De Robertis for *The White Ship*; 1943: *A Pilot Returns*; *The Man of the Cross* (*L'Uomo della Croce*); 1945: *Open City* [B]; 1946: *Paisan*; 1948: *Amore*; *Germany Year Zero*; *The Miracle*; 1949: *La Macchina Amazzacativas*; 1950: *Flowers of St. Francis* [IFC]; *Stromboli*; 1952: *Europa 51*; 1953: *Where is Liberty?* (*Dove e la Libertà?*); 1954: *Journey in Italy* (*Viaggio in Italia*); 1956: *Jeanne au Bucher*; 1957: *Fear* (*Hangst*); 1958: *India*; 1959: *General Della Rovere* [C16]; 1960: *Night in Rome* (*Era Notte a Roma*).

VISCONTI, Luchino (Italian) 1906-

1936: Assisted Renoir on *A Day in the Country* and *Les Bas Fonds*; 1942: Directed *Ossessione* (from *The Postman Always Rings Twice*); 1948: *La Terra Trema*; 1951: *Bellissima*; 1953: "The Lap Dog," an episode *Of Life and Love*; 1954: *Senso*; 1957: *White Nights*; 1960: *Rocco and his Brothers* [IFC]; 1961: "The Job," an episode in *Boccaccio 70*; 1963: *The Leopard*.

WELLES, Orson (USA) 1915-

1941: *Citizen Kane* [B, C, FI, TWF, etc.]; 1942: *The Magnificent Ambersons* [B, FI]; 1943: *Journey into Fear* (signed by Norman Foster) [FI]; 1946: *The Stranger*; 1947: *The Lady from Shanghai* [B];

1948: *Macbeth* [B]; 1952: *Othello*; 1955: *Mr. Arkadin* [C]; 1958: *Touch of Evil*; 1962: *The Trial* [B].

WILDER, Billy (USA) 1906-

1942: *The Major and the Minor*; 1943: *Five Graves to Cairo*; 1944: *Double Indemnity*; 1945: *The Lost Weekend*; 1948: *The Emperor Waltz*; *A Foreign Affair*; 1950: *Sunset Boulevard* [B, FI]; 1951: *Ace in the Hole* [6]; 1953: *Stalag 17* [FI]; 1954: *Sabrina* [FI]; 1955: *The Seven Year Itch* [FI]; 1957: *Spirit of St. Louis* [FI]; *Love in the Afternoon*; 1958: *Witness for the Prosecution*; 1959: *Some Like It Hot*; 1960: *The Apartment*; 1961: *One, Two, Three*; 1962: *Irma La Douce*; 1964: *Kiss Me Stupid*.

WYLER, William (USA) 1902-

1926: *Lazy Lighting*; *Stolen Ranch*; 1927: *Blazing Days*; *Hard Fists*; *Straight Shooting*; *The Border Cavalier*; *Desert Dust*; 1928: *Thunder Riders*; *Anybody Here Seen Kelly?*; 1929: *The Shakedown*; *Love Trap*; 1930: *Hell's Heroes*; *The Storm*; 1932: *A House Divided*; *Tom Brown of Culver*; 1933: *Her First Mate*; *Counsellor at Law*; 1935: *The Good Fairy*; *The Gay Deception*; 1936: *Come and Get It* (with Howard Hawks); *Dodsworth*; *These Three*; 1937: *Dead End*; 1938: *Jezebel*; 1939: *Wuthering Heights*; 1940: *The Letter*; *The Westerner*; 1941: *The Little Foxes*; 1942: *Mrs. Miniver* [FI]; 1943-45: *The Memphis Belle*; *The Fighting Lady*; 1946: *The Best Years of Our Lives*; 1949: *The Heiress*; 1951: *Detective Story* [FI]; 1952: *Carrie*; 1953: *Roman Holiday* [B, FI]; 1955: *The Desperate Hours* [FI]; 1956: *Friendly Persuasion* [IP]; 1958: *The Big Country*; 1959: *Ben Hur*; 1962: *The Children's Hour*.

---

[6] Also called *Big Carnival*.

ZINNEMANN, Fred (USA) 1907-

1935: *The Wave* (co-directed with Gomez Muriel) [B]; 1942: *Kid Glove Killer*; *Eyes in the Night*; 1944: *The Seventh Cross* [FI]; 1946: *Little Mr. Jim* [FI]; 1947: *My Brother Talks to Horses* [FI]; 1948: *The Search* [FI]; 1949: *Act of Violence*; 1950: *The Men* [B]; *Teresa* [B, FI]; 1952: *High Noon* [B, IFC]; *The Member of the Wedding* [IFC]; 1953: *From Here to Eternity* [B, IFC]; 1955: *Oklahoma!*; 1957: *A Hatful of Rain* [FI]; 1959: *The Nun's Story*; 1960: *The Sundowners*; 1964: *Behold a Pale Horse*.

Appendix D

Bibliography

This annotated bibliography is a selection made from among many hundreds of books on films available. Books marked with an asterisk [*] are recommended as being of special value. A brief selection of film journals and critics who might be read with profit are suggested at the end of the bibliography.

1. Bibliography

Leonard, Harold (ed.) *The Film Index, A Bibliography. Vol. I. The Film As Art.* New York: H. W. Wilson Co., 1940. An important bibliography for film research in English. This bibliography is most thorough in its coverage of books, articles and unpublished materials on history, aesthetics and film reviews up to 1939. It concentrates on U. S. films.

Manz, H. P. (ed.). *Internationale Filmbibliographie 1952-1962.* Zurich: Verlag Hans Rohr, 1963. 262 pp. This Swiss bibliography carries Vincent's work [see below] up to 1962. The entries number about 3,000 and give the title in the original language with a brief German commentary. The stress is on Continental film.

Vincent, Carl; Redi, Ricardo; Venturini, Franco (eds.). *General Bibliography of Motion Pictures,* Rome: Edizinni dell' Ateneo, 1953. 234 pp. A bibliographical coverage of books and articles on all facets of film research and background up to 1953. Published in Italy with introductory material for each section in Italian, French and English. The work stresses Continental film.

2. Biography

Griffith, Richard. *The World of Robert Flaherty.*

New York: Duell, Sloan, and Pearce, 1953. A biography employing the journals, diaries and letters of the pioneer of documentary film making. This book gives the reader an insight into what made Flaherty unique in his approach to his subject matter. The respect bordering on adoration that Griffith has toward Flaherty is evident and sometimes colors the book's judgments.

Huff, Theodore. *Charlie Chaplin.* New York: Schuman, 1951. 354 pp. This is probably the most thorough of the English biographies. It is questionable whether Huff does as good a job of capturing the genius of Chaplin as in tracking down all of the important facts of his career. A standard work.

Seton, Marie. *Sergei M. Eisenstein.* New York: A. A. Wyn, 1952. 533 pp. The biography written by a close friend of Eisenstein gives more than just an account of his life. Anecdotes of his work and attitudes toward many subjects help the reader understand the complex nature of the Russian genius. Miss Seton's knowledge of the film itself adds to the authority of what she has to say concerning Eisenstein and other film makers treated in the book.

3. Documentary-Experimental

Hardy, Forsyth (ed.). *Grierson on Documentary.* New York: Harcourt, Brace and Co., 1947. 324 pp. A series of essays by one of the fathers of the documentary movement. Invaluable for gaining an understanding of what philosophies and social attitudes underlay the documentarist's approach to his subject.

Manvell, Roger (ed.). *Experiment in the Film.* London: Grey Walls, 1949. 285 pp. This book contains a collection of essays by different experts all trying to say what the avant-garde movement in films means to *them.* A little confusing but still worth knowing something about.

Rotha, Paul. *The Documentary Film*. London: Faber and Faber, Ltd., 1952 (rev. ed.). 412 pp. A substantial approach to the documentary film, not quite a popular treatment of the subject, but quite readable for one interested in the documentary movement. Rotha brings to this book not only his practical knowledge of film making, but his work as a film historian as well.

4. Education in Films

*Peters, J. M. L. *Teaching about the Film*. New York: International Documents Service (UNESCO Publ.), 1961 (paperback). A good current summary of the place of film study in formal education. This book shows the growing interest in such a project especially among the British secondary schools. The book has a practical value in concentrating its interest on secondary schools, where the need seems greatest at present. Good brief bibliography.

5. Film Criticism

Agee, James. *Agee on Film*. Vol. I and II. New York: McDowell, Obolensky, Inc., 1958 and 1960. A series of film reviews, essays and film scripts by one of America's more memorable film critics and screenwriters. Though much of the subject matter is dated because of the superficial nature of the films reviewed, the Agee volumes have merit in affording the reader the opportunity of reading a highly literate and knowledgeable film critic.

*Bazin, André. *Qu'est-ce que le cinéma?* Vols. 1-4. Paris: Editions du Cerf, 1958, 1959, 1961 and 1962. 178 pp., 145 pp., 181 pp., 163 pp. These four slim volumes represent a good part of the work of a French critic whose influence on contemporary film theory and film making has been outstanding. Since his death in 1958, there has been no one of his stature to take his place. One or more of these volumes are being translated into English.

Donner, Jörn. *The Personal Vision of Ingmar Bergman.* Translated by Holger Lundbergh. Bloomington, Indiana: Indiana University Press, 1964. 276 pp. The most complete analysis of Bergman's films available in English, the book provides much valuable information about Bergman's thirty films. The writer, a young Swedish critic and film maker, gives a picture of Bergman's pictures taken as a whole and not in isolation as they are often treated. There is an extensive bibliography.

6. Film History

*Anderson, Joseph and Richie, Donald. *The Japanese Film: Art and Industry.* New York: Grove Press, 1960. 456 pp. (paperback). A valuable book for understanding the background and major works of the most important Japanese film makers. It is not an easy book to read, but it seems essential to any genuine understanding of the many excellent Japanese films being distributed today.

Fenin, George and Everson, William K. *The Western: From Silents to Cinerama.* New York: Orion Press, 1962. 384 pp. The only book in English to devote a full study to the history of one of America's unique contributions to world cinema, the cowboy. It is more a well ordered report of the facts than a theory of westerns.

Houston, Penelope. *The Contemporary Cinema.* Penguin Books, Ltd., 1963. 222 pp. This is a survey of the main currents of film making since the end of World War II. Besides film makers and their films, Miss Houston traces the vast changes that have taken place within the industry and how films have not only survived the advent of television but in a sense have gained new life from the threat.

*Jacobs, Lewis. *The Rise of the American Film: A Critical History.* New York: Harcourt, Brace and Co.,

1939. 585 pp. A comprehensive history of the art and business of the American film from its beginnings to 1939. Absolutely indispensable reading.

*Leyda, Jay. *Kino: A History of the Russian and Soviet Film.* New York: Macmillan Co., 1960. 493 pp. By far the best history of the Russian film. The post-Stalin period is only briefly treated, but the periods before this, especially the silent films of Eisenstein, Pudovkin and others should be required reading for any serious student of film.

Rotha, Paul and Griffith, Richard. *The Film Till Now.* London: Vision Press, 1949. 755 pp. Still the best book in English for a history of world cinema. The revised edition of 1949 added many pages and stills to the already sizable book. It currently runs over 800 pages.

Sadoul, Georges. *French Film.* London: Falcon Press, Ltd., 1953. 131 pp. About the only book available in English by the outstanding French critic-historian of the film. This volume gives a brief survey of the French motion picture from the turn of the century through the Second World War.

———— *Histoire du Cinéma mondial.* Paris: Editions Flammarion, 1959. 676 pp. In this volume Sadoul has written less a history than an encyclopedia in which he gathers the historical facts about the birth and development of the motion picture in every country from the U.S.A. to the new African nations. Several appendices are valuable sources of facts.

7. Film Theory and Aesthetics

Arnheim, Rudolf. *Film as Art.* Berkeley: University of California Press, 1957. 230 pp. Arnheim's theory is often quite dated and difficult to follow. Most of the essays were written in the 1930's. His approach is primarily psychological.

*Balazs, Bela. *Theory of the Film.* London: Denis

Dobson, Ltd., 1952. 291 pp. An important and quite readable theory of the film written by one of Europe's better theorists and film critics. First published at the beginning of the sound period, it tends to rely heavily on the Russian silent films and is, consequently, influenced in its social theory by the Marxism of that time.

Benoit-Levy, Jean. *The Art of the Motion Picture.* New York: Coward-McCann, Inc., 1946. 263 pp. The author, a film maker himself, gives emphasis to the educational possibilities of film. In the first half of the book, he carefully distinguishes and analyzes the documentary, informational and educational film; in the second half, he deals with the entertainment film, though with the stress on the educative potential of this film genre.

Bluestone, George. *Novels into Films.* Berkeley: University of California Press, 1962. 237 pp. (paperback). This is an academic study of the problem of adapting one medium, the written story, to another medium, the film. After an introductory consideration of the aesthetic problems involved, the author gets down to analyzing six such adaptations.

*Eisenstein, Sergei M. *Film Form and the Film Sense.* New York: Meridian Press, 1960. 279 pp. and 282 pp. (two in one paperback edition). An important series of essays on film theory and film making by one of the great film makers and theoreticians. Often difficult reading but worth any time spent in reading and rereading these pages.

Feldman, Joseph and Feldman, Harry. *Dynamics of the Film.* New York: Heritage House, 1952. 255 pp. A very readable and quite thorough basic study of the techniques of film making. Many examples of movies both American and European are used to illustrate the points.

Fischer, Edward. *The Screen Arts.* New York:

Sheed and Ward, Inc., 1960. 184 pp. In this introductory book, the author is trying to give a general audience some norms for film and television appreciation and criticism.

Hughes, Robert (ed.). *Film, Book I: The Audience and the Filmmaker.* New York: Grove Press, 1959. 158 pp. (paperback). A stimulating series of essays dealing with various aspects of film making and audience appreciation.

————— *Film, Book II: Films of Peace and War.* New York: Grove Press, 1962. 256 pp. A second series of essays gathered by the same editor. These deal with themes of war and peace in films in various countries throughout the world. The quality of the selections varies.

Jacobs, Lewis (ed.). *Introduction to the Art of the Movies.* New York: Noonday Press, 1960. 302 pp. (paperback). A valuable compilation of essays written on the art of the film from the silents to 1960. Naturally some of the essays are better than others, but all are worth reading and many are worth rereading.

Knight, Arthur. *The Liveliest Art: A Panoramic History of the Movies.* New York: New American Library, 1957. 352 pp. (paperback). A popular study of the history of world cinema. Perhaps a bit superficial in places; it nevertheless is a good book for anyone wanting a survey of the movies' history. It covers the silents through the new mechanical processes of wide screen and sterophonic sound.

*Kracauer, Siegfried. *Theory of Film: The Redemption of Physical Reality.* New York: Oxford Press, 1960. 364 pp. The author develops his theory of film through a careful analysis of still photography and then traces two main traditions of film making that may be designated the realistic and the fantasy tendencies. The author opts for the realistic tradition and trys to show why this is the genuine tradition in the light of his analysis. Kracauer takes his place along side of Eisenstein and Balazs as a film theorist of importance.

Lindgren, Ernest. *The Art of the Film*. New York: Macmillan Co., 1948. 242 pp. A good introduction to the art of the film from the point of view of both techniques and aesthetics. The many examples used in the book are drawn from British films for the most part. It is clearly written and quite readable for the beginner.

Lynch, William F., S.J. *The Image Industries*. New York: Sheed and Ward, Inc., 1959. 159 pp. Father Lynch not only points out some of the problems with the mass media of television and film but offers some solutions.

*Pudovkin, V. I. *Film Techniques and Film Acting*. New York: Evergreen Press, 1960. 388 pp. (paperback). An important book of theory and practice written by one of the leading film makers of Russia. An important book for a serious study of the film.

Talbot, Daniel (ed.). *Film: An Anthology*. New York: Simon and Shuster, 1959. 650 pp. The book has all the advantages and drawbacks of an anthology. It contains selections from writings on film from many countries and times. It is a good starting point for the beginner in film aesthetics and theory.

Warshow, Robert. *The Immediate Experience*. Garden City: Doubleday and Co., Inc., 1962. 282 pp. A collection of essays on various aspects of the mass media, written by the former editor and critic for *Commentary*. Falling somewhere between criticism and social analysis, the essays are sensitive and sensible reactions of a man of good taste with a definite set of political convictions to films and their effect on our culture.

8. Production and Technique

Lawson, John Howard. *Theory and Technique of Playwriting and Screenwriting.* New York: Putnam, 1949. 464 pp. This represents one of many possible approaches to the problem of screenwriting. However, the theory of Lawson has added weight because he has been successful as a writer for both stage and screen.

Manvell, Roger and Huntley, John. *The Technique of Film Music.* London: Focal Press, 1957. 229 pp. A competent, recent study of a little-discussed area of the film art. Music is an important factor in the total impact of most films though many critics fail to take this into account in their judgments. This analysis will be helpful for the beginner as well as one more advanced in film study.

Nilssen, Vladimir. *The Cinema as a Graphic Art.* New York: Hill and Wang, 1959. 227 pp. Some rather technical discussion on the dynamics and composition techniques of the camera by one of Eisenstein's pupils. Still of value after almost thirty years (first published in 1936).

*Reisz, Karel. *The Techniques of Film Editing.* New York: Farrar, Strauss and Young, 1953. 288 pp. A study of the most basic component of the art of the film: editing. Compiled and partly written by a distinguished British film director, the book is a careful discussion of editing in relation to mood, story development, rhythm and so forth. Well illustrated and described in language that is not difficult for the beginner to understand (there is a glossary for technical terms).

Spottiswoode, Raymond. *Film and Its Techniques.* Berkeley: University of California Press, 1951. 516 pp. One of the most complete coverages on the technical mechanics of films without being specifically for the expert. However, since the technology involved in filming has changed somewhat since 1951, the book is slightly dated.

9. Screen Plays

A few examples of worthwhile scripts now available to the reading public:

Antonioni, Michelangelo. *Screenplays by Michelangelo Antonioni.* New York: Orion Press, 1962.

Bergman, Ingmar. *Four Screenplays of Ingmar Bergman.* New York: Simon and Shuster, 1960.

Eisenstein, Sergei M. *Ivan the Terrible.* New York: Simon and Shuster, 1962.

Fellini, Federico. *La Dolce Vita.* New York: Ballantine Books, Inc., 1961.

Robbe-Grillet, Alain. *Last Year at Marienbad.* New York: Grove Press, 1962.

10. Social Aspects of the Film

Le cinéma dans l'enseignement de l'église. Vatican City: Polyglot Press, 1955. 558 pp. A collection of documents of the Roman Catholic Church on the subject of films.

Gardiner, Harold C., S.J. and Getlein, Frank. *Movies, Morals and Art.* New York: Sheed and Ward, Inc., 1961. 179 pp. Some ideas on censorship from an expert in the field of literary censorship problems.

The Influence of the Cinema on Children and Adolescents: An Annotated International Bibliography. New York: International Documents Service (UNESCO), 1961. 106 pp. (This and other UNESCO publications available from UNESCO Publications Center, 801 Third Avenue, New York 22, N. Y.) This complete annotated bibliography of articles and books from many countries should give the reader a good idea of the trends in current thinking and research in the important area of the influence of the film on the young.

Klapper, Joseph. *The Effects of Mass Communica-*

tion. Glencoe, Illinois: Free Press, 1960. 302 pp. This book draws together a great deal of material in the complex area of communication research without going beyond its evidence in the final conclusions. A good book to understand the approach of communication research techniques and discoveries.

*Kracauer, Siegfried. *From Caligari to Hitler: A Psychological Study of the German Film.* New York: Noonday Press, 1959. 361 pp. (paperback). A study in social psychology of the German film from the end of World War I until the rise of Hitler. The author concludes that the films of the period indicate the social and political immaturity of the German people and point to the needs of that society which Hitler fulfilled. The book contains an important appendix concerning the Nazi propaganda film.

McCann, Richard D. *Hollywood in Transition.* Boston: Houghton Mifflin, 1962. 208 pp. The author briefly analyzes some of the freedoms that film makers have acquired with the change in the movie industries during the fifties. He also warns of the dangers that these new freedoms bring. A good brief analysis of what happened in Hollywood when TV moved in.

Mayer, Jacob P. *Sociology of Film: Studies and Documents.* London: Faber and Faber, 1946. 328 pp. A study of the attitudes of young people toward the movies and screen personalities. Extensive use is made of the questionnaire method in order to elicit information from the viewers. Some of the conclusions arrived at have become dated, but the book continues to have value in demonstrating one approach to film sociology.

Morin, Edgar. *The Stars.* New York: Grove Press, 1960. 190 pp. (paperback). An analysis of the star system, the influence the stars have upon the audience, the economy and the making of movies. In addition to the general treatment of the star system, attention is given to specific stars like Chaplin and Dean to demonstrate the author's thesis.

Powdermaker, Hortense. *Hollywood: The Dream Factory*. Boston: Little Brown, 1950. 342 pp. An anthropological approach to the film makers in Hollywood. Though much has changed in Hollywood since the book was written, still there is some value in seeing what influenced films at a time when Hollywood was at its peak.

Spraos, John. *The Decline of the Cinema: An Economist's Report*. London: Allen and Unwin, 1962. This study of the British film industry is a sobering reminder that the economics of a mass media industry are vitally important. Some suggestions are made as to how British film makers can receive help from government subsidies.

Wolfenstein, Martha and Leites, Nathan. *Movies: A Psychological Study*. Glencoe, Illinois: Free Press, 1950. 316 pp. One of the few attempts to subject the content of movies to psychological norms of study in book-length form. The book possesses real value in pointing out recurrent themes and attitudes presented in the movies. American, British and French films of the thirties and forties constitute the matter used in the study.

N.B. A note on the "7e Art" series of Editions du Cerf, Paris. This series of books about films and film makers has contributed many stimulating studies during the past dozen years. Among some of the important titles it has brought before the French-reading public (besides the Bazin title listed above on p. 188) these stand out: H. Agel and A. Ayfre *Le cinéma et le sacré*, Rieupeyrout and Bazin *Le western*, Siclier *Nouvelle Vague?* There are over thirty titles currently available.

Journals, Magazines, Critics

The following film magazines might provide a starting point for reading about films: *Sight and Sound, Film Quarterly, Film Culture, Films in Review, The Green Sheet, Screen Education* (British), *New York Film Bulletin.*

The critics that might be sampled or regularly followed: Crowther, *New York Times,* Criste, *New York Herald Tribune,* Walsh, *America,* Hartung, *Commonweal,* Macdonald, *Esquire,* Kauffman, *New Republic,* Alpert and Knight, *Saturday Review.*

Films on Film Appreciation

An excellent series of four, half-hour, 16 mm color films on film appreciation has just been released by OFM Productions. Professor Edward Fischer of Notre Dame University Communication Arts Department begins with the grammar and progresses to the deeper aspects of film, under the following titles: (I) The Elements of Film, (II) The Form, (III) The Nature, (IV) The Spirit.

With the cooperation of such stars as Ann Blyth, Jane Meadows, and Ruth Hussey, demonstration sequences are played to illustrate the techniques of production, and experts from the classics are used freely in Nos. III and IV.

As far as we know, this is the first time that film itself has been used to teach film appreciation.

Explanatory notes and questions for discussion, designed to aid teachers and study groups, are available with the series from OFM Productions, 1229 South Santee Street, Los Angeles, California 90015.

DEUS BOOKS
Popular Paulist Paperbacks

Specially designed to fill the widespread current need for popular treatments of religious and social topics underlying the contemporary scene. Each is timely, stimulating, solidly informative.

THE ADVENT OF SALVATION by Jean Danielou, S.J. Since we say it is possible for those outside the Church to be saved, why do we insist that everyone ought to be a Catholic? 95c

UNLESS SOME MAN SHOW ME by Rev. Alexander Jones. A book to meet the need for Catholic biblical literature, solid in substance yet attractive in form. A surprisingly cheerful book on Old Testament interpretation. 95c

WHAT IS THE CHURCH? by Donal Flanagan. For the interested layman and for the priest who wishes to brush up his theology and to obtain fairly easily a bird's eye view of the fruit of some of the recent trends in ecclesiology. 95c

COMMUNISM TODAY: BELIEF AND PRACTICE by Victor Ferkiss, Ph.D. Presents to the average reader, in non-technical language, a picture of Communism, without bias or distortion. 95c

ECUMENICAL COUNCILS OF THE CATHOLIC CHURCH by Hubert Jedin. A brief and proportioned account for the general reader of the most important previous Councils and the issues they decided. (Available in U. S. only.) 95c

THINK AND PRAY by Joseph McSorley, C.S.P. A series of object lessons for those who are learning the art of communing with God. The central doctrines of Catholicism are covered. For group and private meditation. 95c

HANDBOOK FOR NEW CATHOLICS by Aloysius J. Burggraff, C.S.P. Contains all the "little things" new Catholics need to know which cannot be covered in basic instructions. Ideal gift for converts. 95c

LOVE OR CONSTRAINT? by Marc Oraison, D.D., M.D. An excellent and important work on the psychological aspects of religious education. 95c

CATHOLICS AND ORTHODOX: CAN THEY UNITE? by Clement C. Englert, C.SS.R. A clear and critical examination of the issues that have separated East and West, by a foremost authority on the Eastern Rite. 75c

THE MEANING OF GRACE by Charles Journet. One of the greatest living Catholic theologians discusses the doctrine of Grace, one of the most serious causes of disagreement between Catholic and Protestant theologians. 95c

MENTAL AND SPIRITUAL HEALTH by Frederick von Gagern. A renowned psychiatrist makes clear that a happy life and progress in perfection depend upon recognition of certain basic psychological truths. 75c

THE PRIESTHOOD OF THE FAITHFUL by Emile-Joseph De Smedt, Bishop of Bruges, Belgium. A summary of the role of the laity in the Church, specially significant in view of the present Ecumenical Council. 95c

A RETREAT FOR LAY PEOPLE by Ronald Knox. Monsignor Knox, in his inimitable style, gives a down-to-earth and sometimes startling view of our problems in the only perspective that matters: in relation to the love of God. 95c

HOW TO ADOPT A CHILD by Don Molinelli. A Deus Book original. Tremendously helpful book to guide childless couples along the pitfall-strewn road to adoption. How adoption agencies work, and their requirements. 75c

HANDBOOK OF CHRISTIAN FEASTS AND CUSTOMS by Francis X. Weiser. Combines material from Father Weiser's "The Christmas Book," "The Easter Book," "The Holyday Book." Covers the liturgical year, inspires fruitful celebration in the church and at home. 95c

THE KEY CONCEPTS OF THE OLD TESTAMENT by Albert Gelin. Shows how divine revelation in the Old Testament prepared us for seeing the truth through God's eyes, as it has been possible for us to do since the birth of Christ. 75c

CHARM FOR YOUNG WOMEN by Anne Culkin. The author's well-known Course in Personality Development for high school and college girls, now in book form. $1.00

MEDITATIONS FOR EVERYMAN
Vol. I: **ADVENT TO PENTECOST** 95c

MEDITATIONS FOR EVERYMAN
Vol. II: **PENTECOST TO ADVENT** 95c

Both by Joseph McSorley, C.S.P. The author reminds the reader of the simple yet infinitely dynamic principles taught by Christ, and helps him to progress spiritually through this series of brief daily meditations.

A PRIMER OF PRAYER by Joseph McSorley, C.S.P. Progress in prayer, how to meditate, cultivate recollection, and deal with distractions. 75c

HOW THE CATHOLIC CHURCH IS GOVERNED by Heinrich Scharp. This well-known Rome newspaper correspondent disentangles the complexities of the day to day government of the Church. (Available in U. S. only.) 75c

MARRIAGE GUIDE FOR ENGAGED CATHOLICS by Rev. William F. McManus. Sound and utterly frank, this book is an ideal preparation for married life. For engaged and young marrieds. 75c

OVERPOPULATION: A CATHOLIC VIEW by Very Rev. Msgr. George A. Kelly. A calm examination of a highly controversial issue, presented within the framework of sociology and religion. 75c

PERSONAL PROBLEMS, ed. Kevin A. Lynch, C.S.P. A series of helpful articles on a variety of emotional and religious problems. 75c

POLITICS, GOVERNMENT, CATHOLICS by Jerome G. Kerwin, Ph.D. Dr. Kerwin's thesis is that American Catholics must enter fully the political and social life of the nation.　　75c

WHAT TO NAME YOUR BABY by John and Ellen Springer. A positive approach to Baptism, for future parents. Contains Rite of Baptism, suggested names, etc.　　75c

THOUGHTS FOR TROUBLED TIMES by Walter J. Sullivan, C.S.P. Brief, helpful meditations for busy Catholics, on many aspects of daily living.　　75c

WHAT ABOUT YOUR DRINKING? by John C. Ford, S.J. The renowned moral theologian presents a reasoned, scientific and moral approach to this widespread problem. Excellent for high school and college youth as well as adults.　　75c

DIFFICULTIES IN MARRIED LIFE by Frederick von Gagern. A psychiatrist's advice to achieve a happy married life . . . and to help create through such marriage a bulwark to protect the new generation.　　75c

UNDERSTANDING MARRIAGE by Charles and Audrey Riker. Ideal for Cana Conferences, college marriage courses, family life courses, and parish discussion groups. Helps engaged and young married couples understand themselves and each other.　　95c

EXPLAINING THE GOSPELS by Wilfrid J. Harrington, O.P. A fascinating, scholarly, yet utterly readable account of the four Gospels . . . their formation, background, agreements and differences, authorship, literary construction and theological ideas.　　95c

THE CHURCH AND THE SUBURBS by Andrew M. Greeley. The Catholic Church in America has shifted to the suburbs along with the largest migration in history. An informed, balanced presentation of both problems and opportunities.　　95c

WHAT IS A SAINT? by Jacques Douillet. Like "What Is Faith?" this paperback needs no introduction to the many thousands who cherish the original clothbound edition. 95c

WHAT IS FAITH? by Eugene Joly. A paperback reprint of a clothbound volume that has been very, very popular with readers. 95c

THE SPLENDOUR OF THE CHURCH by Henri de Lubac, S.J. A meditative attempt on the part of the author to work himself, and his readers, into the heart of the mystery of the Church. $1.25

SHAPING THE CHRISTIAN MESSAGE, ed. Gerard S. Sloyan. This book gives special attention to the problems of the "new catechetical movement" of the last fifty years. It incorporates the answers that a number of educators have given to the most fundamental question of our times: how are the young to be formed, and not merely instructed, in accordance with the living message of Jesus Christ? 95c

THE LIFE OF FAITH by Romano Guardini. One of the foremost European theologians of our times analyzes what faith means as an experience in ourselves and others. He examines the relationship of faith to action, love, hope and knowledge, and the Church's part in fostering and preserving the life of faith in each of its members. 75c

JOSEPH THE SILENT by Michel Gasnier, O.P. A historical reconstruction of Joseph's life and a study of his spirituality. In no sense is this a fictional or imaginative work; it follows closely the Gospel narrative and takes into account the teachings of the Church. 95c

FREEDOM OF CHOICE IN EDUCATION by Virgil C. Blum, S.J. A challenging study setting forth the reasons why the State and Federal Government, to be effectively engaged in education, ought to distribute benefits to those who attend private schools. For parents, educators, lawyers and members of the clergy. 95c

MYSTICS OF OUR TIMES by Hilda Graef. This collection of biographies of ten mystics of the past one hundred years shows that a life of spirituality and mysticism can be lived by individuals engaged in the ordinary pursuits of business and living. Each combined contemplation with active lives. Each profoundly transformed the circle in which he or she lived and each is a source of inspiration to modern readers. An original approach to an ever-inspiring subject: the personal life of man with God.   95c

A SELECTION OF CONTEMPORARY RELIGIOUS POETRY, ed. Samuel Hazo. In his choice of poems for this selection, Samuel Hazo shows how mid-century poets—primarily in America—have faced the facts of life within their own age before they refused, accepted or transcended them. The English Departments of high schools and colleges will welcome this book.   95c

WITNESSES TO GOD by Leonard Johnston. The Bible has become so well worn in our civilization there is a need for something to help you see it fresh. This is what this book helps the reader to do. It is written with liveliness and wit, yet with a full weight of expert scholarship behind it.   95c

THE FASCINATING FEMALE by Dorothy Dohen. Every woman, married and single, will recognize the problems discussed by the author and be interested in her suggestions for a happy family life. This book has been written for the American Catholic woman primarily. In it Dorothy Dohen blends psychological, sociological and religious perspective with unusual success. Every woman will want to have a copy.   95c

LIFE AND LOVE: THE COMMANDMENTS FOR TEENAGERS by Daniel Lowery, C.SS.R. This book is meant especially for high school students. The emphasis is that the duties and responsibilities of Catholic living should not be looked upon as just so many "do's" and "don't's". The challenge of the faith is to see how much God has loved us, and to respond to God's love. A splendid text for high school classes in religion.   95c

CHRISTIAN FAMILY FINANCE by William J. Whalen. Drawing upon a wealth of experience, common sense, and detailed professional knowledge, the author discusses home-owning, furniture, credit and installment buying, insurance, food, clothing, recreation, health, taxes, investments, charity, social security and retirement. A book for husbands and wives and all engaged in family counseling. **95c**

COUNCIL SPEECHES OF VATICAN II, ed. Hans Küng, Yves Congar, O.P., Daniel O'Hanlon, S.J. "To praise this collection of 51 Council speeches would be like praising Shakespeare or the Bible. . . . It will undoubtedly become a Catholic classic." **Catholic World** (A Catholic Book Club Selection) **$1.25**

A BIBLIOGRAPHY FOR CHRISTIAN FORMATION IN THE FAMILY by Mother Marie Aimee Carey, O.S.U. This bibliography is intended for parents in order to aid them in fostering a genuinely Christian family life and in fulfilling their responsibilities toward the religious and moral training of their children. It also serves as an excellent guide for religious teachers, directors of Family Life groups in their role of counseling parents of children from pre-school years through elementary school. **95c**

LIVE IN HOPE by Walter J. Sullivan, C.S.P. Stimulating encounters with St. Paul, Cervantes, Sophocles and Newman: these one-page reflections offer adventure among the masterpieces. Essays on **Macbeth, Hamlet, Winter's Tale, Troilus and Cressida, As You Like It,** and **Richard II** afford enticing meditations for a Shakespearean year. All essays are calculated to engender hope.

RETREAT FOR BEGINNERS by Ronald Knox. A series of conferences that Msgr. Knox gave to boys in retreat at school. This book reveals the author's keen insight and wisdom as he speaks directly and forcefully to young men. As has been the case for every one of Msgr. Knox's published works, whether they are addressed to a particular or general audience, this book will appeal to the general reader just as much as it will appeal to young men. **95c**

LITURGY IN FOCUS by Gerard S. Sloyan. How the liturgy is something quite distinct from rubrics, how the Eucharist is at the center of the liturgy, how the sacraments are not just passing events in the life of every Christian, but are daily operative in their lives. No matter what point or problem of the liturgy Fr. Sloyan discusses, each chapter implements the idea that the liturgy is meant to mold and fashion the lives of every Christian, that it is not merely the commemoration of what once existed, but that it is living and real.   95c

A KEY TO THE PARABLES by Wilfrid J. Harrington, O.P. Here are all the parables of the New Testament places in their original setting—the ministry of Jesus. Father Harrington demonstrates conclusively how most of us are surely unaware that the parables, as they stand in the gospels, may not have quite the same meaning they had when first spoken by our Lord. In other words, if we cannot to some extent at least establish the original sense of a parable, it is obvious that we are going to miss something of its true meaning.   95c

ECUMENICAL THEOLOGY TODAY by Gregory Baum, O.S.A. The ecumenical movement is constantly expanding in the Christian world and it is the purpose of this book to explain and analyze the significant events and theological developments associated with this movement. This book consists of 30 articles, each is distinguished by its creative approach to theological questions. This book is divided into five parts: Problems of the Council, The Catholic Church, Ecumenical Developments, Ecumenical Dialogue, Christians and Jews.   95c

A MAN NAMED JOHN F. KENNEDY, ed. Charles J. Stewart and Bruce Kendall. Twenty-five sermons—selected from 850 from 50 states and Washington, D. C.—by the American clergy (Protestant, Catholic and Jew). An eloquent as well as an historical record of the representative words and reactions of the American clergy. (Requests of sermons went to nearly 2,000 clergymen.)
$1.25

A GUIDE TO PACEM IN TERRIS FOR STUDENTS by Peter Riga. Weaving his book with a strong thread of charity, Fr. Riga both instructs and admonishes, touching upon the plethora of problems that plague today's world: unemployment, racism, colonialism, human rights, economic rights, underdeveloped countries, etc. This book does not have to be restricted to Catholic high schools; its message is broader. **95c**

THE LITURGY CONSTITUTION with study-club questions and complete text of the Constitution and **Motu Proprio** of Paul VI. A chapter-by-chapter analysis of the Constitution on the Sacred Liturgy for the many people who may find it difficult at times to perceive the full import of the Constitution. Six authors of special competence, who had been in touch with the liturgical movement for years, divided the Constitution between them, and each took the sections in which he was most competent. Through their combined efforts they provide in this book the liturgical and theological context which the Constitution presupposes and in which its significance is perceived more fully. **95c**

FOUR CONTEMPORARY RELIGIOUS PLAYS, ed. Robert J. Allen. "The Shadow of the Valley" by Jan Hartman, an original 3-part mystery cycle in prose and verse, dramatizing the crisis of faith in the modern world; "Once There Was A Postman" by Robert Crean, a 1-act father-son drama of superb sentiment; "The Broken Pitcher" by Leo Brady, a 1-act drama of conflicting loyalties set in a Red Chinese prison which holds three American Air Force men; "Without The Angels" by Robert Crean, a wacky 1-act comedy, satirizing "pat" religious art. Preface by Pulitzer Prize winning historian-novelist, Paul Horgan. Eight pages of photos from the TV productions of these plays on the CBS and NBC Networks. All plays adapted for stage production. **95c**

UNDERSTANDING PARENTHOOD by Charles and Audrey Riker. An informal and practical handbook about children and their development. **95c**

SOCIAL ASPECTS OF THE CHRISTIAN FAITH CONTAINED IN MATER ET MAGISTRA AND PACEM IN TERRIS by Mother Maria Carl Haipt, O.S.U. Adopted for implementation of the religious syllabus of the New York Archdiocese. Provides background and material and a discussion of concepts basic to an understanding of the Church's social teaching. Aims to open the way to a more enlightened Christian action in our times.   75c

THE ENEMIES OF LOVE by Dom Aelred Watkin. In this meditative and instructive study of the subject of love the author shows that human love (if rightly understood) is divine love translated into the terms of human experience. He examines the assaults which selfishness makes upon that love and indicates where and how they may be overcome.   95c

JESUS: A DIALOGUE WITH THE SAVIOUR by a Monk of the Eastern Church. Sometimes our pretentious and complicated apostolates of today create the false impression that the man of today cannot hear Christ without all kinds of explanations, rearrangements and especially without endless preparation. In this work, however, the author is able to make every man hear Christ from the very first word. In his forty short meditations he recaptures the words and scenes of the Gospel and succeeds in helping us rediscover and appreciate more fully that very springing forth of the Word of God.   95c

THE CATHOLIC QUEST FOR CHRISTIAN UNITY by Gregory Baum, O.S.A. A balanced study of the contemporary movement for Christian unity in the Church and other Christian communities, this work studies the new attitude this movement has produced in the Catholic Church. It will open new vistas for the individual reader who desires to widen his work for Christian unity and will give him a new insight into the Church's ecumenical task.   95c

NOTES

NOTES

NOTES

NOTES

NOTES

NOTES

NOTES

NOTES

NOTES

NOTES

NOTES

NOTES